Monsters of the South

Dedication:
To the witnesses who find the courage to report what they've seen and to the first responders and field researchers who believe them, take their claims seriously, and investigate the sightings of strange and unusual occurrences.

Content Warning: This book contains retellings of historical events. Some include references to suicide, murder, and cannibalism and may not be appropriate for all audiences.

Cover design by Jonathan Norberg
Text design by Karla Linder
Edited by Ryan Jacobson and Jenna Barron
Proofread by Emily Beaumont

All images copyrighted.
Shelley Anderson: 134; **Brianna Royle Koqka:** 135
ADK branding background by **chyworks/Shutterstock.com**
Images used under license from Shutterstock.com:
Covers and silhouettes: **Sergey Arkhipov:** wolf head;
Background and silhouette: hands
Interior: **JM-MEDIA:** 1, 33; **Joeprachatree:** 101

10 9 8 7 6 5 4 3 2 1

Monsters of the South: Stories of Swamp Creatures, Aliens, and Other Legendary Beasts

Published by Adventure Publications
An imprint of AdventureKEEN
310 Garfield Street South
Cambridge, Minnesota 55008
(800) 678-7006
www.adventurepublications.net

Printed in the USA
Cataloging-in-Publication data is available from the Library of Congress.
ISBN 978-1-64755-548-1 (pbk.); 978-1-64755-549-8 (ebook)

Monsters of the South

Jessica Freeburg & Natalie Fowler

Adventure Publications

Table of Contents

Acknowledgments vi

Important Note vii

Preface viii

MONSTER CREATURES OF THE SKY

Little Gray Men (Kelly/Hopkinsville, Kentucky) 3

Moon Man (Kilgore Hills, Mississippi) 11

Snallygaster (Preston County, West Virginia) 15

Mothman (Clendenin and Point Pleasant, West Virginia) 19

Houston Batman (Houston, Texas) 27

Flying Dinosaur of Myrtle Beach (Myrtle Beach, South Carolina) 31

MONSTER CREATURES OF THE LAND

Alabama White Thang (Hurricane Mountain, Alabama) 35

Boggy Bayou Bigfoot (Cotton Island, Louisiana) 39

Skunk Ape (The Everglades, Florida) 45

Chatawa Monster (Chatawa, Mississippi) 49

Georgia Werewolf (Woodland, Georgia) 53

Wild Wolf Woman (Mobile, Alabama) 59

Fouke Monster of Boggy Creek (Fouke, Arkansas) 63

Glutton / Santer (Statesville, North Carolina) 69

Demon Dog of Valle Crucis (Valle Crucis, North Carolina) 73

Bunny Man (Clifton, Virginia) 77

Green Hill Monster (Talihina, Oklahoma) 81
Flintville Monster (Flintville, Tennessee) 85
Beast of Okefenokee Swamp
(Okefenokee National Wildlife Refuge, Georgia) 87
Rougarou (Terrebonne Parish, Louisiana) 93
Lake Worth Monster/Goatman
(Greer Island, Texas) 97

MONSTER CREATURES OF THE WATER
White River Monster (Newport, Arkansas) 103
St. Augustine Sea Monster
(St. Augustine, Florida) 107
Lizard Man of Scape Ore Swamp
(Bishopville, South Carolina) 111
"Normie" the Lake Norman Monster
(Lake Norman, North Carolina) 115
Lake Herrington Monster
(Herrington Lake, Kentucky) 119

Bibliography 124
About Jessica Freeburg 134
About Natalie Fowler 135

Acknowledgments

We want to thank the witnesses who report their stories. We understand how vulnerable it can feel to share an unusual experience with others. Without your courage, these books wouldn't be possible. Your bravery in speaking up plays a vital role in keeping these legends alive.

We also want to extend our gratitude to the first responders and investigators who took these reports seriously, recognizing that even the most extraordinary encounters deserve attention. Your dedication to understanding and preserving the truth—no matter how strange—is deeply appreciated.

Finally, a heartfelt thanks to all the readers who approach these tales with open minds and a sense of curiosity. Your enthusiasm for the unknown inspires us to keep writing!

Important Note

Curiosity sometimes leads people to go out looking for ghosts and monsters, but please respect the law, as well as the rights and privacy of others.

Most importantly, we ask anyone who investigates the paranormal to exhibit extreme caution. Do not take this lightly. Tragically, people have died while pursuing legends. Your life is precious, and it is not worth risking. If there is any danger, please, let the legends remain as legends.

Furthermore, the information provided in this book is for reading entertainment purposes only. The authors and publisher do not assume and hereby disclaim any liability to any party for any loss, damage, or disruption caused by any other use of this information.

Preface

The South is unlike any other region in our country. From vast swampy areas like the Everglades to the lush, forested foothills of the Appalachian Mountains, it's no wonder the southern states have some of the most well-documented and credible cryptid and monster stories in the United States—so many, in fact, that it was difficult to choose which accounts to include here.

As paranormal investigators, we wish that we could personally investigate every one of these stories for ourselves. We are grateful for those who have reported their experiences with care and precision. Using those reports, we were able to recreate their encounters in a narrative style that's intended to allow you, our readers, to feel the witnesses' tension, fear, and shock.

So, sit back, settle in, and enjoy. We are excited to share some of the most tantalizing monster stories from this region that's ripe with terror. From the clear skies to the murky waters, keep your eyes open. And never mind that screech you just heard outside your window. It's probably just a bird.

—Jessica Freeburg and Natalie Fowler

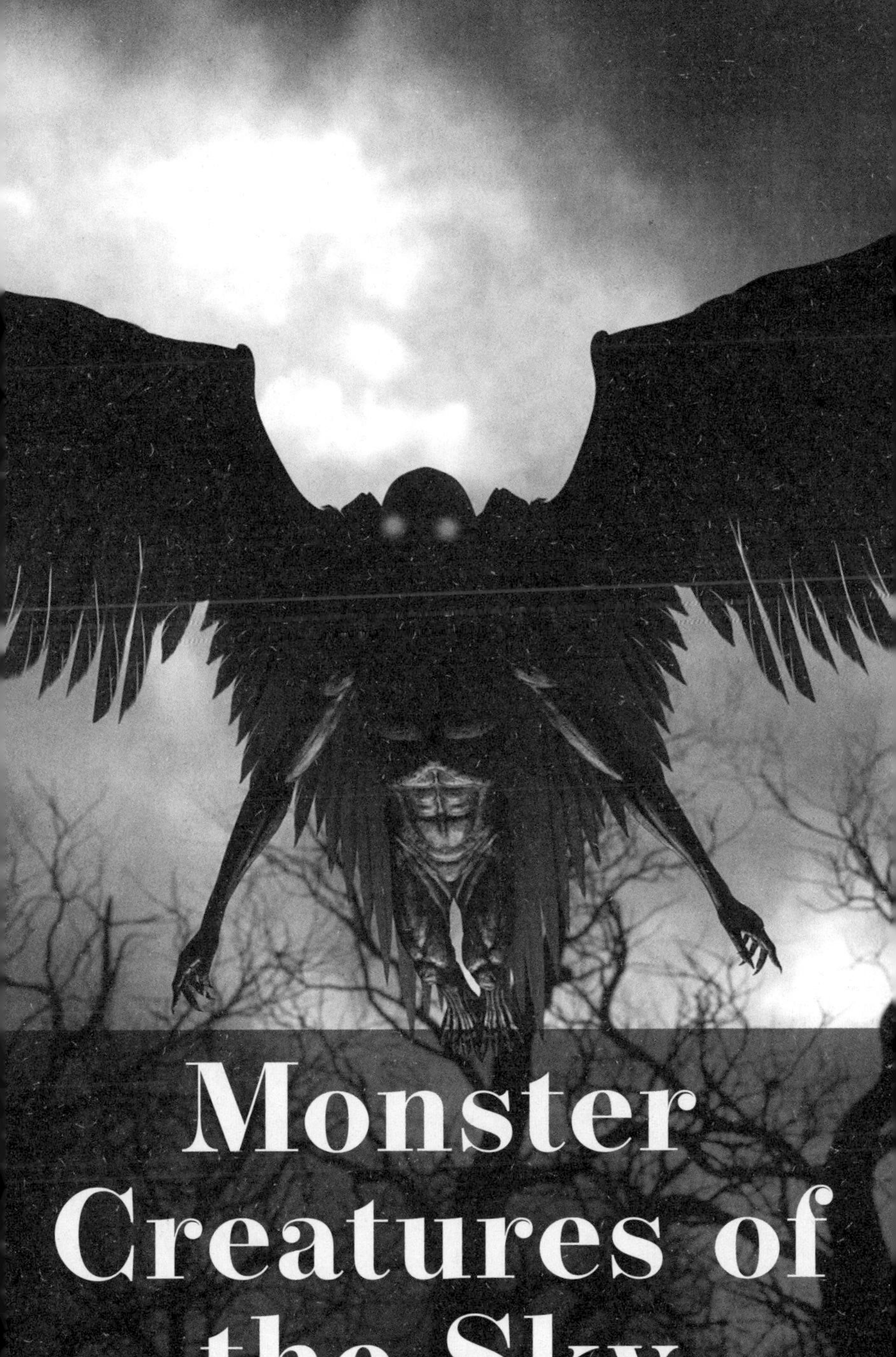

Monster Creatures of the Sky

Little Gray Men

Kelly/Hopkinsville, Kentucky August 21, 1955

"Here you go, Mama," Mary said, handing her mother a large bowl.

"Thank you, sweet girl," Glennie replied, smiling down at her youngest child. Glennie filled the bowl with lettuce from the garden and tossed some sliced tomatoes and cucumbers into the mix.

Her daughters-in-law, Vera and Arlene, set out plates and utensils, along with the pot of freshly cooked sweet corn. It was a feast. With children ranging from 7 to 25 years old, 50-year-old Glennie was thrilled to have everyone together on this steamy Sunday evening.

The small three-room house was about as filled with friends and family as it could get. Along with Glennie's oldest sons—Lucky and J.C.—and their wives, her three younger children—Lonnie, Charlton, and Mary—were there. Arlene's brother O.P. and Lucky's friend Billy Ray and his wife, June, had also joined them for the evening.

"Dinner's about ready," Glennie called out. "We'll need someone to fetch water from the well out back."

"Happy to," Billy Ray said.

The screen door banged shut behind him as he hurried out. Rounding the side of the house, he walked briskly toward the well.

As he pulled up the bucket of water, Billy Ray was startled to see a saucer-shaped object fly silently across the horizon. Behind it, a trail of exhaust cut a rainbow-colored line across the early evening sky. The object flew slowly over the house before coming to an abrupt stop above a forested area just beyond the farmstead that dropped into a 40-foot gully.

Billy Ray was intrigued and a little frightened. He couldn't find any logical explanation for what he'd just seen. He hurried back inside and announced, "I just saw a flying saucer in the backyard." He hoped the others wouldn't notice the slight tremble in his voice.

For a moment, everyone was silent as they gaped at him.

"Sure ya did," Lucky replied, breaking the silence.

Snickers rippled through the small kitchen, as the children resumed putting food on their plates.

"I swear, I did," Billy Ray implored, his voice rising a level. "It looked like an egg-shaped washtub, barreling through the sky."

"I think you've read one too many copies of *Fate* magazine," J.C. said.

"I'm telling ya—" Billy Ray began.

"Hush now," Glennie interrupted. "All this nonsense about UFOs is going to scare the children." She handed Billy Ray a plate, the look on her face a firm warning that she wasn't having any of it. "Get yourself some food."

Billy Ray accepted the plate and did as he was told. Perhaps they were right. Talk of UFOs had been rampant in the area over the past few years. Maybe he was mistaken. He actually wanted to believe he was wrong. The idea that a UFO had just landed nearby scared him more than he wanted to admit.

Day fully gave way to dusk. The group of family and friends finished dinner and settled around the living room. Billy Ray let himself believe the object he'd seen was nothing more than a figment of his imagination—until the casual conversation and laughter was interrupted by the family's dog, barking furiously outside.

Lucky stomped onto the back porch. Billy Ray followed. The dog, still barking wildly, rushed toward them and scurried under the porch. The men saw a strange glow, moving slowly amid the trees where Billy Ray had seen the saucer descend. A moment later, they realized that the glowing object was moving toward them.

As the bright sphere of light drew closer, they saw that the eerie glow emanated from a small, man-like being, roughly 3 feet tall with metallic gray skin. The creature seemed to look directly at them with large yellow eyes the size of small plates. The two eyes were set wide apart on a smooth, bulbous head.

"What is that?" Lucky exclaimed.

"It's gotta be from the UFO I saw," Billy Ray replied, his voice tight with fear.

Lucky darted inside and grabbed his 20-gauge shotgun. On his way back out, he handed Billy Ray a .22 rifle. The men were used to handling guns. They ate what they hunted and would also defend their loved ones if something, be it man or beast, threatened them.

The creature continued coming forward. Long arms hung on either side of its body, nearly dragging on the ground. It seemed to lack knees, which caused its hips to move awkwardly, as the motion of its thin, straight legs propelled it forward— nearly human-like but not quite. The odd creature raised its arms above its head. Slender, talon-like fingers cast spindly shadows across the yard.

Although the creature's stance seemed to indicate a sort of surrender, the men were too frightened to ask if it came in peace. Lucky cocked the shotgun and took aim. Billy Ray did the same. The men shot at the unwelcome visitor. However, the being simply did a backflip, then darted back into the cluster of trees from which it had emerged.

Lucky and Billy Ray backed into the house, keeping their eyes on the tree line.

"I don't think our bullets hurt it," Billy Ray said, horrified.

"What's happening?" Glennie asked, her three younger children gathered around her, their eyes wide.

"Something came out of the woods," Lucky replied.

"An alien from the UFO I saw," Billy Ray added as June rushed to his side.

"Did you kill it?" she asked.

"No," Lucky said, his thin voice illustrating his fear. "It scurried back into the trees."

Arlene looked toward the windows, uncertain whether she believed what she was hearing. The landscape outside was dark. Reflections of those gathered in the living room looked back at her like wide-eyed ghosts—bewildered and afraid.

"Mama, hide the young'uns," J.C. said, pointing toward the bedroom.

Glennie calmly led the children down the hallway and instructed them to get under the bed.

"Everything will be okay," she assured them. "You just wait here."

The men stood in the living room, watching and waiting. It wasn't long before a bald, metallic-colored head with two large ears looked into the house through one of the windows. The men took aim and fired through the screen. The creature fell backward but quickly stood and hustled away.

Billy Ray bolted through the back door to chase the creature. But as he stepped outside, a hand reached down from the roof, grabbing his hair.

June threw her arms around his body and pulled him back inside. "They're on top of the house," she cried.

Lucky ran outside and shot the creature on the roof. His bullet met its target with a loud ting, as if hitting metal. The creature fell off the roof and scrambled away.

"There's another one in the tree," Billy Ray yelled.

Lucky and Billy Ray opened fire. Their bullets hit the strange beast with metallic clangs. The force of the bullets knocked the creature from its perch. Oddly, it seemed to float gently toward the ground. More bullets rained down upon the alien, sending it rushing away just as the others had.

The others stood inside, watching in horror through the windows as another creature came around the side of the house, its arms extended above its head. It was oddly shaped, with a thick chest and no neck—like nothing they'd ever seen before.

"It looks like a 5-gallon gasoline can with a head on top and small legs," Glennie observed. "Do you think it's trying to communicate?"

The creature was just feet from Lucky when he pulled the trigger. Again, his bullet seemed to ricochet off the silver-coated beast before it rushed away. Clearly, shooting the creatures was of little use. The family retreated into the home, turned on the porch lights, and waited, watching out the windows while protecting the doors.

The tiny humanoids continued to climb on the roof and peer into the windows, then scurry away after being shot at. This went on for several hours.

"I don't know how much longer we can keep shooting at them like this," Lucky said.

"We've gone through a few boxes of bullets, and they're still coming at us." Billy Ray added.

Throughout the evening, Glennie had remained calm, quietly observing the behaviors of the odd entities. She had drawn the conclusion that they were curious and, although relentless, weren't aggressive toward them.

"They haven't tried coming into the house at all. They just keep looking in at us," Glennie noted. "Maybe they don't want to hurt us. I say we load up the cars and go into Hopkinsville to get the police," she said.

Everyone agreed, and the family was able to get into their vehicles without incident. They sped into town and arrived at the police station around 11 p.m., clearly distressed. The story they shared was beyond belief, but officials were inclined to believe them. They were not the kind of people who made up tall tales—or often reached out to authorities for help. They were people who worked hard and took care of their own, on their own.

"What do you make of this?" one of the officers asked police chief Russell Greenwell.

"These people are genuinely terrified," the chief replied. "Billy Ray's heart rate is twice the normal rate."

"There's no signs that any of them have been drinking," another officer added. "They're as sober as a church organist on Sunday morning."

Twelve local police officers, along with four military police officials, drove to the homestead. One of the officers reported seeing two meteors traveling away from the site of the attack. The grounds were searched for several hours, and the family remained outside, unwilling to go into the house until the police made certain that none of the creatures were there.

"Have you found anything?" Chief Greenwell asked as a few officers returned from the outlying field.

"We found a luminous patch, about 1¼ feet in diameter, on the ground right around where Lucky said he shot the thing."

"I saw a greenish glow in the trees, but we investigated and couldn't find a source," another officer reported.

"They clearly had a shootout here," the chief surmised, eyeing a hole in the screen door. "Whatever it was, it scared these folks something fierce."

By 2:15 a.m., the initial investigation had concluded. The traumatized family and friends settled into the living room for the night and tried to sleep. But at 3:30 a.m., Glennie awoke to a pair of bright eyes looking in at her, clawed fingers pressed against the window.

"They're back," Glennie whispered.

Lucky jumped up, his gun in his hand. "Mama, I'm gonna shoot that little man!"

"It won't do any good."

Her words fell on deaf ears. The cycle of shooting the creatures, watching them flee, and waiting for them to return started up again. It went on for another hour or so before the small gray humanoids finally seemed to leave for good.

We may never know for certain what Glennie and her family encountered that fateful evening in 1955. But their account would go down as one of the most notorious alien encounters in history. Their description of the little gray men, misrepresented as "little green men" in newspaper accounts, became the foundation for the stereotypical alien as we know it today.

These oddly shaped little fellows who seemed more curious than dangerous inspired one of the most famous aliens of all: a lovable little creature called E.T., who delighted audiences on the big screen nearly three decades after the harrowing encounter on a farm between Kelly and Hopkinsville, Kentucky.

Moon Man

Kilgore Hills, Mississippi 1883

Gus Goode eased the horse to a stop next to his friend and neighbor Byron Thompson, who sat in his saddle, looking across the cotton field at the horizon.

"I don't think we're going to find your mare before the sun sets," Gus said.

Byron just stared with his mouth open.

Gus followed his gaze and looked to the sky.

"You see that, right?" Bryron asked, pointing toward a valley near the edge of his field.

Speechless himself, Gus could only nod.

The men watched as something soared across the sky. It glowed, lighting up the darkening night just as the sun sank lower.

Gus had heard strange accounts of things in the sky for the last several weeks, but he didn't comprehend what his neighbors were talking about. People had described it as a ship, a boat-looking object—but in the sky. It was like the world had turned upside down and the sky was the ocean. That wasn't something he'd been able to understand, until now. As he observed the strange phenomenon with his own eyes, he didn't have quite the right words to explain it. "Ship" was the best way he could think to describe it.

"Let's go see what it is," Gus finally said.

Byron slid his rifle out of its tether and secured the weapon around his shoulder, just in case. Gus did the same.

The pair rode for several minutes. They urged their horses along, a little faster. Gus felt his breath quicken, and his heart rate increased. The closer they got to the glow, the more his brain struggled to make sense of it.

As they neared the bright light, they slowed their horses, silently agreeing that they perhaps shouldn't be pursuing this strange anomaly. Twigs and underbrush crunched underneath the horses' hooves; the sound made Gus nervous. He motioned for Byron to stop. Without a word, he dismounted, and Byron did the same. They secured their horses to a tree and stepped lightly the rest of the way.

The men saw the source of the light at nearly the same time. A large, barrel-shaped object sat in an open clearing. The area around it was lit up like daytime. Several creatures, about 5 feet tall, walked around the mysterious object. Their large, cat-like eyes sparkled in the bright light emanating from the strange container.

Byron raised his rifle and fired several shots, transforming the odd-yet-quiet scene into deafening chaos. The strange, inhuman creatures rushed to a door in the barrel-shaped vessel. Before the men knew what was happening, the craft rose into the sky, using some strange magic, the likes of which neither of them had ever seen.

"What in the Sam Hill . . ." Byron's voice trailed off as he watched the ship shoot across the sky and disappear from sight.

Gus and Byron dove for cover. When the sky was quiet, they slowly stood up.

"Should we go look?" Byron asked.

"We have to," Gus whispered.

Together, they walked to the spot where the ship had been.

"You hit one," Gus said, his voice tight with excitement.

The men ran to the motionless form lying on the ground. The creature's chest rose and fell one last time as life left its body.

"It's dead," Byron said in awe. "Look at that gray skin. It's so odd, almost like a little human in some ways."

Gus poked it with a stick. "It has the skin of an elephant. I don't know . . . it's like the man from the moon fell right out of the sky."

"What should we do with it?" asked Byron.

The men looked around and then up at the sky. Whatever it was, the others might return for their fallen brother. But the sky was empty, and the world around them was surprisingly calm.

"Let's take it back to my saloon," Gus suggested. "Other people need to see this, or they'll never believe us."

The men transported the fallen creature to town and placed it on a cot on the front porch of the Big Springs Saloon. For days, it drew a crowd of curious spectators who could have their picture taken with it for $5—a steep price for a photograph at the time. But soon the decaying corpse began to stink. The odor was enough to keep most of the curious-minded folks away. The men begrudgingly accepted that their strange trophy could no longer be kept on display.

"Why don't we bury it?" Gus suggested. "We can make a little graveyard for it—and for any other moon men if they happen to come around this way again."

No other moon men were ever buried alongside the fallen alien. The location of the burial site has been lost to time, yet the legend lives on.

Snallygaster

Preston County, West Virginia
Summer 1951

Charles wasn't sure how long he'd been asleep before something snapped him out of a dream. He bolted upright in bed, instinctively straining to listen. As he became more fully awake, he registered a sound.

Clunk-clicketa. Clunk-clicketa.

It was the sound of something heavy moving along his rooftop.

Clunk-clicketa. Clunk-clicketa.

It moved directly above him—each step a plod of weight, followed by the tap of what Charles quickly surmised to be talons.

"A bird, maybe," he said to himself, "but a real big one."

His thoughts were disrupted by a loud screech—like the whistle of a locomotive but shriller, if that was possible. His breath caught in his throat. That was no bird. Not a normal bird, anyway.

He slid out of bed and reached beside his nightstand, grabbing his shotgun. He'd lived in the Appalachian highlands of West Virginia all of his life. He was familiar with the sounds of the creatures that called the thick forests home, and he'd heard that screech before.

The first time, he was just a boy, checking coyote traps with his older brother and Grandpappy on the outskirts of his grandfather's property. They'd heard the flapping of giant wings. When they looked up, they saw something out of a nightmare. Four clawed legs hung below a thick, reptile-like body covered in grayish-green scales. Its wings spanned no less than 30 feet, and it must have weighed at least 800 pounds. A long, sharp beak—that looked strong enough to tear a man apart—spread open as it screeched wildly.

"*Schnelle Geist,*" Grandpappy said in awe. He grabbed Charles and his brother by the backs of their shirts and pulled them behind a tree.

Those two German words, meaning "quick ghost," were first spoken by German immigrants in the 1700s, when the strange beast was first seen. Sightings of the creature became so prevalent at the turn of the 20th century that President Theodore Roosevelt even wanted to hunt and kill one.

Charles wrapped his arms around Grandpappy's leg, fearful that the creature might choose him for dinner. He'd heard stories of the beast that locals nicknamed the snallygaster, and he knew, according to the stories, that it was particularly fond of feasting on poultry—or children. Charles shuddered at the thought.

The creature had its eyes on something else. It swooped toward one of their traps, where a coyote, its leg caught tightly in the steel jaws, lay whimpering in the dewy grass. The snallygaster grabbed the coyote, sinking sharp, 6-inch talons into the unfortunate prey's torso and forcing a howl from the poor animal's mouth. The snallygaster screeched, drowning out the coyote's sorrowful cries, and it rose upward, yanking the trap out of the ground. The 2-foot anchor dangled below the chain as it swayed below the coyote's lifeless body.

The snallygaster glided toward the forest and disappeared into the treetops. One last screech echoed through the dense woodlands before the scene returned to silence.

The memory of that encounter played quickly through Charles's mind as he strode to his bedroom window. The beast took one last step on the roof above him, and then Charles heard the wings cut through the air before he saw the creature swoop toward his barn.

His suspicions confirmed, he pushed the window open and pointed the barrel of the shotgun. He glanced at his barn, filled with animals he raised—a few pigs and a mess of chickens. He looked toward the small pasture just beyond, dotted with calves, many of them just starting to wean off their mother's milk.

Charles eyed the large six-pointed star, painted just above the hayloft door—a bright contrast of yellow, blue, orange, and green against the weathered red paint on the barnwood. It was more than a decoration; it was a hex sign: a symbol of protection that was meant to keep his livestock safe.

Charles cocked the hammer on his shotgun and readied himself. If the hex sign didn't stop the snallygaster, he would stop the beast himself. As the creature neared the barn, it bellowed a wicked cry before making a wide swoop. Then, changing course completely, it flapped back over Charles's house.

Charles ran from his bedroom, the shotgun still braced against his shoulder as he opened the back door and stood on the porch. He watched the snallygaster glide high toward the tops of the mountainous woodlands beyond his property and disappear into the darkness. There, Charles stood a while longer, watching to make sure the monster didn't return.

He was thankful the snallygaster had changed its mind as it approached the barn. It seemed the hex sign had served its purpose. Leading up to that night, he'd often second-guessed himself for painting the symbol. Now, he wondered how many nights it had prevented catastrophe.

Mothman

Clendenin, West Virginia
November 12, 1966

Kenneth Duncan drove his shovel into the hard earth with a force he didn't know he had. It had been a long few weeks, watching his father-in-law waste away into nothing. His wife sat with her father, waiting for the end; Kenneth was happy to finally have some way to help—even if it meant digging Homer's grave.

"You don't have to be here," his friend Robert said.

"Yeah, we can handle this," Emil agreed. "Go on home to your wife."

"I want to be here," Kenneth answered simply, digging at the ground again. It was as if all the built-up emotions could pass through his arms, into the shovel, and down into the ground as he dug. It felt good to release them.

After scooping a few more shovels of dirt, he stopped. He was tired. The sleepless nights had taken their toll. He rested his elbows on his shovel and looked up. That's when he spotted it. A large black creature lifted out of the trees. It had the general shape of a human but was very long—probably taller than a man.

Completely speechless, Kenneth could only watch, his eyes fixated on the massive being's outstretched wings. The strange man-bird glided effortlessly through the sky, drifting out of sight.

The shock that had crippled Kenneth's speech finally faded. "Did you . . . see that?" he gasped, unable to find his words very quickly.

"See what?" asked Emil.

"The black birdman," Kenneth replied.

The others stopped digging to stare at him.

"I think you should get on home," said Robert. "Get yourself some sleep."

Kenneth slowly nodded and handed over his shovel. "Maybe I'll go sit by that tree for a minute."

"You do that," said Emil. "We've got this."

Point Pleasant, West Virginia
November 15, 1966

Linda and Roger Scarberry and Mary and Steve Mallette were driving near the abandoned National Guard Armory on State Route 62, just north of Point Pleasant, at about midnight.

"Look, over there," said Linda. She pointed to the old power plant near what everyone referred to as the TNT area.

A 7-foot-tall creature stood on top of the bunker, glaring at their car.

“What is that?” Steve asked, his voice filled with surprise. “It’s like a man but with wings.”

“Look at its red eyes,” Mary noted, worriedly.

“Those eyes,” agreed Linda, “they’re glowing. I feel like they’re trying to hypnotize me.”

“Let’s get out of here.” Roger whipped the car around and sped back toward Point Pleasant.

Linda looked out the back window and saw the bird-like creature swoop over the car.

“Oh, no,” she cried, “it’s following us.”

“Where did it go?” Mary asked.

“There,” shouted Linda. “It’s up there!” She pointed toward the sky.

To their horror, it remained above the car, effortlessly gliding above it. When the two couples safely reached town, they could no longer see the monster.

“Where do you think it is?” Roger asked.

“I don’t know,” Steve replied.

Roger turned and began driving back to the armory.

“What are you doing?” asked Linda, not bothering to hide the fear in her voice. “You’re going back to find it again?”

“I want to see if it’s still there,” Roger replied.

“Yes, good idea,” Steve agreed, with what sounded like more confidence than he felt.

They didn’t wait long to get their answer.

“It’s still there,” shouted Mary. “Look!”

“It was waiting for us to come back,” Steve said, mystified.

They all watched as the black birdman ran toward them, clumsily, through the field.

“Now can we go?” begged Linda, her voice tight with terror.

Roger turned the car around again, and they raced back to town and called the police.

Over the next several months, many others reported seeing what came to be known as the Mothman, named after a villain in the Batman cartoon. Two volunteer firemen and a contractor were among those who reported it, describing the creature as a large bird with red eyes that glowed like reflectors.

November 15, 1967

"Mama, how long does it take to get to Grandma's?" asked 5-year-old Gwendolyn. She was perched in her usual spot: on her knees in the middle of the backseat, looking out the back window.

Gwendolyn's mother smiled. Every Friday afternoon, they drove across the Silver Bridge to eat dinner with her mother in Kanuga, Ohio. And every week, as soon as they had gotten through the traffic signal and had driven onto the bridge, Gwendolyn asked the very same question.

Her mother gave the very same, very expected answer. "Oh, Gwenny, you know. We go over the river and through the woods, to Grandmother's house we go." She sang the last part—as she always did—stretching it out until they got to the end of the bridge.

In the backseat, Gwendolyn burst into a fit of laughter, the way she always did. But, today, her giggles stopped abruptly. "Oh, mama!" she exclaimed.

"Yes?" her mother asked, glancing into the rearview mirror.

"Look!" She pointed out the back window.

"Tell me, dear. I'm driving, and I can't look."

"It's a big, black birdman—standing on top of the bridge!"

Her mother turned and tried to look, wondering if her daughter was the latest witness to the infamous and legendary Point Pleasant Mothman.

* * *

Charlene Clark Wood sighed and patted her pregnant belly. "We'll be home soon, little one," she said to her stomach. Charlene was tired after spending the day on her feet, working at the salon, and she was especially tired of waiting in the line of traffic to cross the Silver Bridge.

She was surprised at how many people were out and about. But then again, it was Friday night, and Christmas was just around the corner. There were presents to buy, trees to get, and grocery shopping to do. She'd just have to wait her turn like everyone else.

The light turned green, and she pressed the gas pedal in her brand-new 1967 Pontiac. As she ventured onto the bridge, she heard a loud boom. The bridge began to shake violently.

Her father, a riverboat captain, had told stories her whole life about barges that hit piers and bridges. Without hesitation, Charlene slammed her car into reverse and accelerated backwards. In seconds, the spot where she'd been on the bridge was gone. Before her eyes, countless tons of metal, debris, cars, and people plummeted into the water.

Hers was the car closest to where the bridge had collapsed. In shock, she sat in her car, unable to move until there was a knock on her window.

"Ma'am, let me help you."

The man was State Patrol Officer Rudy Odell. He opened her car door and led her out. Another man, Robert Rimmey, took an arm, and they walked her carefully off the bridge to safety.

The air was filled with sounds of people screaming. Charlene scanned the scene in front of her and attempted to process it. Wires dangled everywhere. Some cars were smashed, twisted, and pinned between layers of metal. Other cars slowly sank into the water below. The cold air bit through her thin winter coat.

* * *

"Mama," Gwendolyn said with a yawn.

"Yes, dear?"

"Why aren't we home yet?"

"There's a lot of traffic tonight, sweetie."

Her mother shifted the car into park. They hadn't moved in several minutes. She was trying to figure out why the traffic in her lane had stopped completely and why no traffic was coming toward her.

"I want to go to my bed."

"I know. You can curl up on the backseat," her mother suggested.

Ahead, Gwendolyn's mother could see that the driver had gotten out of his car and was standing on the road. "I'm going to see what's going on. You stay here."

She opened her door, climbed out, and could immediately hear screams coming from the river.

The man in front of her turned around. "The bridge is out. It's . . . gone," he said weakly.

The reality of the carnage that she and her daughter had narrowly escaped registered in her brain and settled into the depths of her soul. She remembered her daughter telling her she'd seen the Mothman on the bridge. Had it been an omen of this terrible tragedy that was about to happen? Was the creature a harbinger of death?

People would ask those questions for decades to come. The curious sightings and tragic disaster created one of the most enduring legends of the 20th century.

Houston Batman

Houston, Texas
June 18, 1953

Judy had been tossing and turning all night. It was hot, and the humidity was stifling. She finally gave up on sleep altogether and ventured onto the porch of her mother's boarding house to wait for her mother to get home from her night shift. To her surprise, she wasn't the only one.

"It's a beautiful night," Hilda commented, leaning back on the porch swing, causing it to sway gently.

Hilda and her husband, Lloyd, had moved into the boarding house just three months before.

"Well, technically, it's morning," Judy noted. At age 14, she was 9 years younger than Hilda, but the two hit it off after Hilda moved in.

Judy sat beside Hilda on the swing. Her mother, Vivian, would be home soon. She generally arrived at around 2:30 a.m.

Howard peeked his head out the front door. "You two can't sleep either?"

"Nope," Hilda replied with a smile. "You're welcome to join us."

Thirty-three-year-old Howard worked as an inspector at a nearby tool plant. He had come to think of Judy as a little sister. Vivian was an attentive landlord who gave off a motherly vibe to her tenants, regardless of their age.

"It feels a few degrees cooler out here," Howard said, settling into a rocking chair.

Silently, Judy agreed.

"There's a nice little breeze," Hilda replied.

As the three sat quietly, enjoying the peace of the early morning, a large shadow moved over the front lawn.

Judy saw the outline of wings cast clearly across the grass.

"Did a moth just fly across a streetlight or something?" asked Hilda.

"I don't think that's a moth," said Judy quietly. She stared at the shadow's source, standing near the pecan tree about 25 feet away.

"Do you see that?" Howard asked, pointing at the same tree.

A man, at least 6½ feet tall, stood on a large branch of the tree. He appeared to be dressed in tight-fitting black clothes with large black wings extending from his back, folded in at his shoulders. He was surrounded by a strange yellow glow. Balancing on the limb, the odd fellow swayed as he observed the housemates.

The three were silent, frozen in shock. This was like nothing they'd ever seen before. Slowly, the glow began to fade, and the figure vanished before their eyes.

Judy's scream broke through the silence. A loud swoosh followed, as something moved quickly over the roofline of the homes across the street. A bright flash of white light illuminated an elongated object that rocketed from a tree and flashed through the sky.

At that moment, Vivian ran up the walkway to the front porch. "Did you see that white flame?" she asked. Her shallow, rapid breaths betrayed her fear. "It looked like a burning paint brush shooting across the sky."

A light trail of smoke was all that remained on the horizon as the four looked up, stupefied.

The next morning, Hilda filed a police report. Within a few hours, the story was front-page news—not the sort of attention that any of the witnesses wanted. They felt foolish to admit what they saw, but they held firmly to their accounts. Another tenant of the house confirmed that he also saw the strange, winged man in the tree that night, but he'd simply gone back to sleep.

Had a half-man, half-bat creature slipped into our dimension for a moment on that fateful evening? More than seven decades later, what it was (and why it was there) remains a mystery that haunts and delights Houstonians. It's likely that the legend of the Houston Batman, as it came to be called, will live on for many generations to come.

Flying Dinosaur of Myrtle Beach

Myrtle Beach, South Carolina Summer 2004

Calleigh watched out the car window. She and her boyfriend, Leo, had just passed through a tiny town that had barely more than a gas station, a bar, and a church. Now they were speeding along the forest road, pine trees lining both sides.

"Thanks again for getting off the highway," she said with a yawn.

It was dark. They had left Roanoke late that afternoon and were finally closing in on their destination: Myrtle Beach.

Leo laughed. "I'd rather take longer to get there than worry about you freaking out about the interstate. Besides, I don't mind the backroads. It's all about the journey, right?"

She smiled and looked at him, but her smile quickly disappeared. Something was flapping right outside his window—as if someone's bed sheets had been hanging out to dry and blew off the line.

Calleigh's mind raced to recognize what she was seeing. There were too many trees for it to be someone's laundry. No, it was something flying, something with huge wings, something that resembled a pterodactyl.

She screamed, "Go, go, go!" She felt certain it was coming for them, and she was afraid it might kill them.

Recognizing her terror, Leo punched the gas.

Later, they stopped to look at the car. A slimy, grayish-green blob of goo—like something from a bad sinus infection—was smeared across the driver's side door. Leo tried to wipe it away, but it wouldn't come off.

"This is crazy," Calleigh said. "What do you suppose it could be?"

He shrugged. "I don't know. Whatever it is, I can't get it off."

In the years that followed, Calleigh and her boyfriend eventually broke up. To her knowledge, he sold the car with the goop-smear still on it. The strange substance never came off the car's window.

While she might have lost touch with Leo, she would never forget that frightening encounter. Was the creature a prehistoric beast that had somehow survived into the modern era? Had the couple experienced some sort of a time slip? These were questions they would never answer.

However, one thing was certain: Something large left its mark on their vehicle. Calleigh only wishes that she had gotten a sample of the paranormal green goo.

Monster Creatures of the Land

Alabama White Thang

Hurricane Mountain, Alabama
Winter, Early 1930s

The old wagon bumped down the road, its wooden wheels creaking under the weight of its heavy load of firewood. James sat atop the wagon seat, holding tightly to the reins. The journey from his home in Rabbittown to Jacksonville was one he'd made many times before. Although the distance was 10 miles, Hurricane Mountain rose up between them, making the scenic trek take longer.

James didn't mind. The city square in Jacksonville was a prime spot to sell firewood. Nights had been chilly, and folks would certainly need kindling. He'd passed by a few Fords coming through Rabbittown. A "Brewster Green" Ford Model A, just like the one he'd been eyeing at the local dealership, had sped around him outside of town, spooking the horses a bit. He saw far more cars than horses and buggies these days. It seemed to him that fast cars and horses didn't mix well. Since the road through Hurricane Mountain was lightly traveled, he stuck to it for these trips.

The afternoon in Jacksonville was productive. The locals cleaned out his supply, just as he'd hoped they would. By the time he sold his last bundle of firewood, it was late in the afternoon, and the sun was already beginning to drop toward the tree line on the horizon. He climbed onto the wagon seat and steered the team back the way he'd come.

As he neared Hurricane Mountain, James considered taking the road around it. But that road was more heavily traveled than the mountain pass. He worried that, in the darkness, his horses could be hit by an oncoming vehicle. There were no houses on the mountainside and almost no one coming or going on the steep, winding road. Sure, it would take him longer, but safety trumped speed.

He'd been making the steady climb up the hill for a while, when he heard the distinct sound of footsteps crunching on dry leaves in the trees beside him. He pulled the reins, bringing the horses to a stop. As the wagon wheels creaked to a halt, the sound of the footsteps stopped with them.

James peered into the trees. What little moonlight might have brightened the sky was nearly choked out by the forest around him. The darkness was oppressively thick.

Seeing nothing out of the ordinary, James gave the reins a light snap, and the horses trudged ahead. The moment their hooves clopped against the road, the leaves began crunching again.

Something was trailing them.

The thought made a shiver run down James' back. He glanced into the forest—but again he saw only darkness. He looked at his horses for any signs of distress. They didn't seem spooked in the least.

"Must be some lost dog," James reasoned aloud.

He pulled the reins once more, curious to see what the footsteps would do. The horses stopped. The crunching leaves stopped. An eerie silence fell around him—the kind of quiet that was completely unnatural in a densely forested area at night. He strained to notice any sign of life but heard only the dull buzz of nothingness.

The silence was suddenly broken by the sound of pounding feet. They were making their way toward the wagon. James's heart nearly jumped into his throat when he saw an 8-foot-tall creature running toward him on two legs. It looked like a very large person, covered in long white hair from head to foot. A stench—reminiscent of dead fish mixed with rotted carcasses—wafted toward him. The beast's eyes glowed red in deeply set sockets and glared at him as it jumped into the front of the wagon.

Horrified, James dove into the wagon bed.

He'd heard stories from locals about a strange woodland creature known as the White Thang. It was known for the horrific sound of its wails, which reportedly were a mix between a screaming woman and a dying cat.

When he turned to look toward the front of the wagon, James saw the creature calmly sit in the seat, take the reins, and give a snap for the horses to move ahead. They complied, as if nothing were out of the ordinary.

For 10 minutes, the wagon continued its assent up the winding road. James huddled like a frightened child in the back of his own wagon, while a wild, hairy beast controlled the reins. When the cart came to the intersection of another road, the creature leapt from the wagon and rushed into the cover of the woodlands.

Bewildered, James hurried into the seat and gave a quick snap of the reins. "Go on," he called to the horses. He glanced over his shoulder toward the trees, his heart racing.

Nothing was there.

James kept the horses moving at a fast pace. He listened carefully the entire way home for any sign that he was being followed, but his stalker had clearly moved on.

James never again traveled the road through Hurricane Mountain, not even in the daylight. Those woods held proof that the local lore was more than just the idle gossip of bored farmers and imaginative children. The Alabama White Thang was real.

Boggy Bayou Bigfoot

Cotton Island, Louisiana
August 22, 2000

"Alright, Carl, let's get back to cutting," Earl said, adjusting his cap.

The morning was already hot, and the pair had taken a break to grab a drink of water to cool off.

"Yes, sir," Carl replied with a nod. He grabbed his chainsaw and strode toward the massive hardwood he'd been focused on prior to their break. He pushed the hand guard forward, squeezed the throttle trigger, and jerked out the starter grip with a short, fast pull. As the saw coughed to life, Carl flipped the master control lever with his thumb, holding the powerful tool with the ease of a man who'd handled a steel chainsaw more hours than he could count.

Earl was a foreman with Delrie Wood Products of Colfax. He'd been with the company for several years and understood the dangers of the job. Staying safe meant staying focused. He enjoyed working with Carl, an experienced saw-cutter who'd also been with the company for years.

Earl had a reputation for leading one of the top crews in the business—a reputation he'd earned with hard work and professionalism. He took pride in doing things well, and he counted on the men on his crew to take equal pride in their work. When Delrie tasked him with removing hardwood logs in the Cotton Island area, he was happy to have Carl take on the work alongside him.

As the men's saws echoed through the densely wooded forest, quick movement in Earl's peripheral caught his attention. He turned to face the movement, his chainsaw idling in his grip.

Earl hit the kill switch on his saw and stared in awe as a 7-foot-tall, bipedal creature, covered in black fur, made its way across an open patch of land. Its long strides carried it quickly away from the men and toward a line of trees.

When Earl's saw went silent, Carl's attention was pulled away from the trunk he'd begun to cut. Looking up from his work, he followed Earl's gaze toward the trees—then flipped his own saw's switch, returning the forest to silence.

The men watched, mouths gaping and eyes wide, as the beast splashed across a nearby creek, its large feet kicking up a spray of water and mud. The creature turned and looked at Earl before regaining its momentum and disappearing into the woods.

"That was Bigfoot," Carl said, breaking the silence.

Earl squinted into the shadows, trying to see where the creature might have gone. Had it kept going? Or was it lurking somewhere beyond sight, watching them, just as they had been watching it? The thought sent a shiver down his spine.

They told Joe Delrie, the owner of the company, about the encounter. The phrase "sins of the father" played through Earl's mind as he shared the experience with his employer.

Some 25 years earlier, Earl's father had been embroiled in a Bigfoot controversy. A teenager at the time, Earl paid little mind to the rumors that swirled around town. It seemed that his father and a friend were testing out a new saw one afternoon, when they decided to have a little fun. They used the saw to cut a piece of plywood into the shape of a large foot, and they left a trail of prints before falsely claiming that they'd discovered proof of Bigfoot.

Earl feared that his boss, a man he had great respect for, would think he was repeating the same kind of prank. Perhaps, if he'd witnessed the spectacle alone, he would have kept it to himself—but Carl had seen it too.

To their relief, Delrie didn't question their account. "You've both been honest and reliable," he told them. "If you say you saw Bigfoot, I believe you."

Earl felt anxious about returning to work the next day, but it turned out to be business as usual. There were no strange creatures to report—none that he noticed anyway. He did feel like he was being watched, but that could've been his imagination. After all, seeing something so out of the ordinary had a way of making even a rational man a little paranoid.

August 24, 2000

It had been two days since Earl and Carl saw the strange creature. Earl had almost put the idea of seeing it again out of his mind, as he and Carl walked the perimeter of the property, surveying the next area they would be clearing.

As his eyes scanned the thicket of trees and underbrush, Earl nearly choked on his own breath. "There he is again," he said to Carl, his voice a hoarse whisper.

Carl stared in stunned silence.

"Hey, there!" Earl hollered. "Get on outta here!"

The creature looked up, fixing its eyes on the men. Its back seemed to straighten as it locked eyes with Earl. It was an imposing figure, looming large among the trees, just a few yards away.

"You heard me!" Earl yelled with more courage than he felt. "Go on. Git!"

The beast turned and lumbered away until it was out of sight.

The men hurried back to the truck and called Delrie.

"I need you to come down here," Earl said. "We saw that booger again."

When Delrie arrived, the three men walked to the area where the creature had been seen.

"I'll be damned if those aren't Bigfoot tracks," Carl said, pointing into the soft soil of the dried-up bog. The large tracks were separated by 6½ feet.

"No human has a stride that long," Delrie noted. "We've got to report this to the sheriff."

Earl didn't necessarily want to tell everyone what he'd seen. He knew firsthand how a man's reputation could be tarnished by stories of Bigfoot. But rumors were already spreading around town about something with sharp claws and big teeth tearing up local farmers' pigs. What if this beast was responsible? The community needed to be on the lookout.

The loggers weren't the only ones to report seeing the elusive creature. A local fisherman had a similar encounter. He claimed the creature gave off a putrefying odor.

Earl and Carl's accounts would reach far beyond the local community. Newspapers in surrounding states shared their tale—many with a layer of doubt and almost all mentioning Earl's father's Bigfoot prank. CNN even published a story from a local reporter.

Hundreds of people descended upon the area. A Bigfoot enthusiast even left a sign, with the property owner's permission, proclaiming the space to be a "Bigfoot Protection Area." Although local law enforcement was determined to treat the sightings as a hoax, local residents weren't so quick to dismiss the stories. For a while, parents kept their children indoors, and local farmers temporarily suspended evening livestock feedings to avoid any late-night encounters with the creature.

Carl and Earl stood firm, never wavering in their account.

"They can say it was a camel riding an elephant," Earl told a reporter. "But I saw what I saw."

Skunk Ape

The Everglades, Florida
July 19, 1997

John Vickers sat up straight and worked a kink out of his neck. He'd been driving the tour bus through the Everglades for some time. He was accustomed to the natural life that roamed along the sides of the roads and sometimes put on a show for his passengers. Alligators, herons, and turtles were among the most common animals to see. An occasional wild boar or white-tailed deer would also make an appearance.

As the bus rolled toward Turner River Road, one of the most scenic routes in the area, something tall—covered in thick, dark hair—strode across the roadway 200 yards in front of the bus. From the moment it came into view until it disappeared into the thicket of cypress and hammock trees, it stood upright on two legs, like a human, only it was not.

For a moment, John thought perhaps it was a bear. But bears don't naturally walk on two legs, like this creature did. As a long-time resident of the area, John was familiar with the local lore about the Skunk Ape. He knew witnesses had reported seeing it in this region for decades, maybe longer.

The name was derived from the uniquely grotesque odor that eyewitnesses commonly reported: a mix of rotten eggs and old cheese. Some speculated that the creature (or creatures) absorbed sulfur from alligator dung as they hid in the marshes. Locals reported hearing the creatures knock on trees and let out an ear-piercing screech at night.

The pit that formed in John's stomach, as his mind raced, was a mixture of excitement and fear.

A passenger tapped lightly on his shoulder. "What was that?"

"Aww, it's probably just the old man who lives out here," John said, trying to conceal the shock that lingered just beneath the surface of his lie.

"I don't think that was a man," a woman said from a row not far behind.

Whispers rippled through the tour bus like a cottonmouth cutting a path through the swampy water. John knew it wasn't an old man or a bear that he'd seen. It was a living, breathing legend. Or it was someone pretending to be one—someone brave enough or dumb enough to plod through the Everglades in the name of a prank.

July 21, 1997

Jan Brock pressed gently against the accelerator as she cruised down the road away from her home. It was

7:45 a.m., and she was heading to the real estate office where she worked.

Something large emerged from the trees and brush lining the side of the road.

"Is that a bear?" she wondered as the creature plodded across her path.

It was roughly 7 feet tall, covered in dark hair, and walked on two legs. The beast continued lumbering upright into the line of trees as she passed it.

"What on Earth...?"

It was unlike anything she'd ever seen before. Jan shuddered and drove on, bewildered and feeling quite uneasy.

* * *

Not long after Jan encountered the unusual creature, her neighbor, Fire Chief Vince Doerr, drove down the same road. When he saw a figure crossing upright ahead, he quickly assessed it was neither a bear nor a man.

He accelerated to the spot the creature had just crossed. Then, after pulling to the side of the road, Vince grabbed the camera he kept in his vehicle and jumped from the truck.

"Hey!" Vince shouted toward the beast.

It turned to face him for a moment, before continuing on its way. Vince snapped a quick photo before the creature disappeared from view. He hurried to have the film developed.

When he got home that evening, he saw Jan in her front yard. He walked to Jan, the newly developed film in his hand. The two made small talk for a few minutes before Vince finally worked up the courage to tell her what was on his mind.

"I saw the strangest thing on the road," he said, opening the photo envelope and pulling out the image of the odd creature.

Jan's mouth dropped open, and her eyes widened. "I saw the same thing," she said, a sense of relief washing over her. "I thought I was losing my mind."

After swapping details about their experiences, they realized they'd seen the same creature just minutes apart.

Did they have a mythical neighbor living in the marshy forests near their homes? Or was the legendary Skunk Ape just passing through? Either way, they had witnessed something that many people have wondered and whispered about over decades, even centuries. Few have actually been lucky enough to see it.

Chatawa Monster

Chatawa, Mississippi
Fall 1902

Grace sat on the stiff chair and tried not to cry. She had to be brave. Her parents were paying a lot of money for her to attend this school. She just wished it wasn't so far away from her family, especially her older brothers.

"My name is Elizabeth," whispered the girl sitting next to her.

Grace smiled. "I'm Grace."

"How old are you?" Elizabeth asked.

"I'm 12. How old are you?"

"I'm 14," said Elizabeth.

The girls were quiet for a minute. Grace was afraid to talk. The nuns scared her, and she didn't know all the rules yet.

Elizabeth reached over and grabbed her hand. "It's going to be okay," she said. "We can be friends."

Grace felt better knowing she already had one friend.

The door opened with a creak. Sister Sarah walked in and strode to the desk in the corner. She smoothed out an invisible wrinkle in her black habit and smiled at the girls.

"Anne will be here in a minute to show you to your rooms," she said.

Grace heard footsteps in the hallway and watched to see if it would be Anne, but it was another nun. Grace had never seen so many nuns in one place before.

"Sister Sarah," said the nun, hurrying to the desk. "It's back. The large monkey in the woods," she hissed. "It's back again."

"Hush now, Sister Margaret," Sister Sarah scolded. "Mind yourself, please. We've got new arrivals." She nodded at the two girls waiting in the chairs.

Grace hadn't known Sister Sarah very long, but she'd never heard her use that tone of voice. She decided that she never wanted to hear it again, especially directed at her.

"I'm sorry," Sister Margaret replied in a whisper, her eyes focused on an invisible spot on the floor.

A tall girl entered. "Hello, Sister Sarah and Sister Margaret. I'm here to take the girls to their new rooms."

Sister Sarah nodded. "Go ahead then."

Grace followed Elizabeth and the person she assumed to be Anne out the door.

"I will show you around first," said Anne. "I'm sure you had a tour with your parents, but it's always nice to see it again."

As they walked up the stairs, Elizabeth asked the question that was burning in Grace's mind. "What did Sister Margaret mean about the giant monkey in the woods?"

Anne glanced around, then waved the girls to a window on the landing. She pointed out to the woods behind the school building. "About 10 years ago, a circus train was passing through town, on the way to New Orleans."

Grace looked out the window, already worried about where the story was going.

"This wasn't just any circus. This was a circus filled with strange and unusual creatures. The most interesting and unusual creature of them all was the half-man, half-ape. He was the star of the show, but he was fierce and extremely dangerous. He'd attack anyone who came near, so they kept him locked in a cage with thick iron bars inside his own railcar."

"His own railcar?" asked Elizabeth skeptically.

Grace could tell by her tone that she doubted the story.

"Yes, anyway, the train crashed and most of the animals were killed—but not the monkey man. They found neither head nor tail of him."

Grace swallowed hard.

"Then someone saw him lurking, right out there in our woods," Anne continued. "So, the townspeople organized a search party to capture him. But they couldn't find him—so don't wander off," she whispered dramatically. "Someone once wandered off . . . and never came back." Anne turned on her heels and marched up the stairs.

Elizabeth waited until Anne was far enough ahead before she whispered, "Don't worry. I'm sure that's just a story they tell to scare us into staying right here, where our parents put us."

Grace nodded. She agreed with Elizabeth—but she wasn't planning to take any chances. Besides, if Sister Margaret saw the monkey man, maybe there was some truth to it.

Georgia Werewolf

Woodland, Georgia
1860s

John stood over a mangled sheep carcass, looking across the pasture at a dozen others in the same condition. Bending down, he studied the damage that had been done to the poor animal. Its white fur was drenched in the browning crust of dried blood. Something had ripped the defenseless creature to shreds, its flesh torn apart. Entrails, ripped from its stomach, lay beside the remains on a patch of blood-soaked earth.

A farmer, hardened by the toils of raising livestock, John swallowed back bile that rose in his throat. These animals had suffered a brutal death. On top of that, his livelihood depended upon keeping them alive until it was time to sell or butcher them.

"I'm heading into town to inform the sheriff," he told his wife, who stood several yards back from the gory scene.

"What could have done such a thing?" she wondered aloud.

"A wolf, maybe a pack of them?" John replied.

He saddled his horse and rode the short distance into town. When he arrived at the sheriff's door, he found a half dozen other men there. Their voices were tight with frustration as they spoke over one another.

"I lost more than 20 sheep last night—and 10 the night before," one man said.

"We're down three cattle now, thanks to this beast," another added.

"It killed every last one of our chickens," a third man declared.

"Gentlemen, calm down," the sheriff said. "We need to keep our wits about us if we want to stop this thing. Wolves are wily creatures when they're hungry. We'll need to outsmart it."

A wagon rumbled toward the crowd, its wheels crunching the dirt path as it rolled to a halt. A young man cleared his throat, causing the crowd to look toward him. An elderly gentleman slouched in the seat beside him, as if his back might break if he tried to straighten it.

"It's not an ordinary wolf," the young man declared. "We've got ourselves a werewolf to stop."

"A werewolf?" the sheriff asked, the word thick like molasses on his tongue. He shook his head. "There's no such thing."

"You can lie to yourself, sheriff," the old man said. His voice sounded like his throat had been worn down by sandpaper. "But this lot would be fools not to listen."

The rumbling of voices in the crowd fell silent.

"We had a similar rash of killings back in Europe," the old man continued. "We stopped that monster the only way you can stop a werewolf."

The men seemed to hold their collective breath, awaiting his next words.

"We melted our silver, made bullets, and shot the wicked creature under the light of the full moon."

"Nonsense," the sheriff grunted.

"Maybe so," one man agreed, "but what have we got to lose by trying? We can't let this go on any longer."

* * *

Several nights later, as the full moon hung brightly in the evening sky, Emily Isabella Burt walked quietly from her bedroom and slipped out the front door of her family home. She had returned from boarding school in England to live with her widowed mother, Mildred.

Emily's mother had managed to raise her four children and maintain the plantation after her husband's death several years earlier. He'd left her with a substantial inheritance, but she had to work hard to maintain the property in a profitable fashion—something few women of that era got the opportunity to do. Mildred was resourceful and strong-willed, traits that served her well over the years and which garnered her much respect from everyone in her community.

Emily was struggling with insomnia, which she thought was caused by her recent travels. But enough time had passed that any lingering effects should have subsided. Still, she couldn't rest at night but found that late-evening walks helped to soothe her spinning mind.

Mildred Burt worried about her daughter's late-night outings. It was strange, to say the least, for a young woman to go out alone after dark—and it certainly wasn't safe. On this evening, Emily's mother decided to go out and search for her daughter. She had heard the rumblings around town about a wild animal killing livestock. She feared that her shy and timid daughter could stumble upon the beast and find herself in grave danger.

As she walked along a trail, looking for her daughter, Mildred heard the voices of men in the distance. They sounded angry and frightened.

"There it is!" a voice shouted above the others.

Gunshots rang out, followed by the loud howl of an injured animal and more frantic voices.

"I hit it," someone said. "But it ran away."

Mildred could hear the chaos of men talking over one another and running through the underbrush of the surrounding forest. Gradually, the sound softened as the men hurried away in search of whatever they'd hit. Mildred hoped they had killed the beast that was terrorizing the community. The thought of some creature ripping animals apart made her shiver with fear.

As she rounded the corner of the trail, Mildred saw a figure lying in the bushes just off the path.

"Emily," she gasped, dropping to her knees beside her daughter.

"Mother," Emily said, her voice weak.

Mildred helped Emily to her feet. As she slipped her shoulder under her daughter's arm, she felt a thick wetness. She looked at her daughter's hand to see blood. A bullet had ripped through her palm.

"Dear Lord, you've been shot!"

She helped Emily back to their home and sent for the doctor. He was able to clean and stitch the wound.

It wasn't long before word had spread around town, and rumors began to swirl. After all, Emily had been shot at the same time the posse of men had shot the werewolf. There were whispers that Emily was morphing into the beast when she went out for her walks and would shift back into her human form each morning. The fact that the nightly livestock massacres stopped after Emily was shot didn't help matters.

Emily Isabella Burt forever after became known as the Georgia Werewolf. Whether she actually was or not remains a mystery.

Wild Wolf Woman

Mobile, Alabama
April 1, 1971

Caroline set the cup of coffee down next to her friend Barbara just as the phone rang. It was early, and the pair had a busy day ahead of them, getting stories ready for the local newspaper.

Barbara mouthed, "Thank you," to Caroline and picked up the phone. "Mobile Press Register," she said into the receiver.

Diligently, she started to scribble notes. At one point, she looked up at Caroline. The look in her eyes told Caroline that she couldn't believe what she was hearing.

Caroline peered over her shoulder and read out loud, "Wolf woman?"

"You don't say?" Barbara said and kept writing. "Is there anything else you'd like to tell me?" she asked after getting the caller's name and phone number.

When the caller finally hung up, Barbara looked up at Caroline. "Well, that was one of the strangest calls I've ever taken."

"What was that about?" asked Caroline.

"They said they saw a wolf woman. Her top half was a beautiful woman, and her bottom half was a wolf." Barbara paused, as if to let that sink in. "They said she was both pretty and hairy." She burst out laughing.

Caroline laughed too. "I hope that's the only crazy one we get."

But it wasn't. Over the next week, roughly 50 phone calls came in with similar sightings. Several reports were called into the police department, as well. On April 8, the newspaper ran with the story.

* * *

"Antoinette," said her father, "I need you to go to your grandmother's house. She has something for me."

Antoinette's eyes grew wide with fear. Normally, Antoinette loved walking to her grandmother's, who lived just around the corner. A lot of friends lived in her neighborhood, and she never had a problem walking to their houses either—but not tonight. Tonight, the sun had just set, and Antoinette didn't want to walk anywhere alone in the dark. Not with the wolf woman on the loose.

Antoinette didn't disclose her fears to her father, but she went to find her mother. "Do I have to?" she asked.

"Of course you have to," said her mother.

"What if she's out there?" Antoinette whispered.

"The wolf woman?" her mother laughed. "Don't be silly. That was just someone's April Fool's joke that got blown out of proportion."

Antionette was quiet. Someone at school had said that someone else's dad had seen the wolf woman, and she had followed him all the way home. No one's dad would make up a story like that.

Antionette left the house and bravely walked to the end of the driveway. She held her head high and, in doing so, held herself together. But as she continued by the patch of woods, something rustled in the brush. Antoinette was sure that she saw something move.

Maybe it was the darkened figure of something big enough to be half woman and half wolf, watching her from the shadows. She wasn't sticking around to find out. All the courage that she had mustered evaporated in a split second. She ran as fast as she could the rest of the way to her grandmother's house. When she had secured the item and caught her breath, she decided there was no sense in delaying the inevitable. She sprinted all the way home again.

"It was just my imagination. It was just my imagination," she repeated to herself until she believed it.

Fouke Monster of Boggy Creek

Fouke, Arkansas
May 1971

Elizabeth Ford's husband, Bobby, had gone hunting with his brother Don and friend Charles. Elizabeth sat curled up on the couch in the front room of her new house, waiting for her husband to return. She had spent the day with Patricia, Don's wife, but it was getting late, and Patricia had gone to bed. Despite feeling exhausted from a week of unpacking, Elizabeth tried to stay awake—but the move had taken its toll, and she drifted off to sleep.

A noise startled her awake. Disoriented, she struggled to remember where she was. She heard a deep, raspy breath inhale and exhale. Her nose wrinkled. A stench wafted into the room. A chill rushed through her veins, and her breath caught in her throat.

Out of the corner of her eye, she saw the curtain rustle. A hand reached through. At first, she thought it belonged to a bear, but it had long scraggly hair. Her eyes followed the arm up to meet the beast's gaze. She stared into its bright-red eyes, and it stared back.

Elizabeth screamed.

* * *

Bobby breathed in the night air. He'd taken his brother and their friend Charles on a tour of his new property, and they'd done a little hunting. The first of many excursions, he hoped.

Bobby put his arm around his brother. "Thanks for your help today."

Don patted his back. "This land is amazing. You're lucky to have found it."

"Do you think Elizabeth will like it in Fouke?" Bobby asked.

A scream echoed through the night, interrupting their conversation.

"Elizabeth!" yelled Bobby. He ran toward the house, shotgun in hand.

Don and Charles followed.

Behind Bobby, one of the men shined a flashlight at the house. Bobby could see something on the porch. It was big, tall, and walked upright.

Together, the men chased it behind the house, firing shots at it. The beast seemed to disappear into nothing.

"I think I hit it," yelled Charles. "I think it fell over there." He pointed toward the treeline.

"Let's go see," said Don.

From behind them, they heard another scream from someone in the house.

"I'm going to check on them," Bobby told the others.

He moved quietly back to the house. If something was there, he wanted to surprise it. He found a ladder behind the house that he'd used earlier in the day. He leaned it carefully against the porch so he could avoid using the obvious stairs. Carefully, he climbed up the first few rungs.

Before he reached the top, he noticed the creature's labored breathing behind him. A long, hairy arm grabbed his shoulder and yanked him back. Together, he and the beast rolled to the ground. He saw the creature's bright-red eyes.

Terrified, all he could think about was how to get away from the monster. "Help!" he shouted.

Bobby broke free of the creature's grip. He scrambled to his feet, ran up the porch steps, and burst through the front door to safety.

* * *

Charles and Don began searching for tracks or blood along the edge of the woods.

"Help!" shouted Bobby.

Together, the men ran back to the house. Charles found Bobby's gun lying in the grass and picked it up. When they went inside, they found Bobby pacing back and forth. He told them what had happened.

"Let's go look," said Don, encouraging Bobby to come back outside.

Charles handed him his gun, and the men ventured onto the porch.

"Look," Charles said, "over there." He pointed to the fields.

From the porch, the men watched as something tall ran upright into the fields. They aimed their weapons and shot.

"It moves fast," Don noted.

"What is it?" asked Bobby.

"I don't know," Charles replied. "But I think it's time to call for help."

It wasn't long before Ernest Walraven, the constable of Fouke, arrived. The men waited while the constable searched the property and surrounding woods. After an hour, Ernest came back to the house.

"I don't know," he said. "Whatever was here before isn't here now." He thought for a minute. "I'm going to head out, but you can keep my shotgun and flashlight as added protection. I'll come back and check on you in the morning."

The men agreed, and the constable left. The men listened to gravel crunch under the constable's tires as he drove away.

* * *

When Ernest got another call, he couldn't say that he was surprised. He climbed the porch steps to the house for a second time that night.

"You have to believe us," said Don, handing the constable his flashlight.

"We shot at it again," said Bobby. "But it's like it just disappears."

The constable nodded once, not sure how much he should say. Instead, he took the opportunity to examine the house more closely. He shined his light at the scratch marks on the window frame. It looked like they'd been made by something with three claws.

He thought for a minute. "You should know that you aren't the only ones."

"What do you mean?" asked Charles.

The constable didn't answer. Instead, he headed down the porch steps to continue his examination in the yard. The men followed him to the dirt, where he used his light to highlight large footprints. It appeared as if the creature only had three toes.

"A few years back," he said, "a lot of people in the Jonesville community reported something similar."

"Like what?" asked Don.

"They said it was a 7-foot, naked man, covered in brown hair."

The constable glanced at Bobby, who'd reported wrestling with the creature during their first sighting. He had gashes from the incident that were still bleeding.

"I think you need to be seen for your injuries," he said.

Bobby was treated at St. Michael's Hospital in Texarkana for shock and for "deep claw marks."

* * *

When officials visited the Fords' house later the next day, they found the couple packing a trailer with all of their belongings. They moved away, never to return.

A few weeks later, three residents of Texarkana called officials to report an incident on US 71. They were driving at night, just south of Fouke, when they almost hit a "giant monkey" that ran upright across the road. They stopped to see what it was, but they realized it had disappeared.

In June, a farmer from Boggy Creek called to report several unusual tracks that he'd found in his soybean field. The game warden, constable, and sheriff measured the tracks and reported that they were 13.5 inches long and 4.5 inches wide. The tracks only had three toes.

Glutton/Santer

Statesville, North Carolina
Fall 1890

Mrs. Chamber rounded the curve along the walkway to her home after visiting Mr. Parks. She had only been gone for an hour, but she had a litter of puppies at home, and one hour was as long as she dared to leave them alone—especially with all the talk around town.

Everyone was abuzz about a creature they were calling the Glutton—a name that had been chosen because of its insatiable appetite. It reportedly carried off grown hogs and cattle, and it was especially fond of dogs and cats. Rumors swirled that it had even killed children, although Mrs. Chamber didn't know anyone who could say whose children.

"Rumors," Mrs. Chamber mumbled to herself.

As she neared the house, she heard a commotion. It was the sound of something heavy rushing across the porch, mixed with the whining of a pup. She hurried toward the noise.

Suddenly, she found herself face-to-face with the beast everyone was talking about. It was large, covered in gray fur, with a feline-like appearance. But it was much bigger than a cat, with long legs and large back feet that resembled bear paws. It was a nasty thing, and it had one of her beloved puppies in its mouth. The creature slinked under the porch. The tufts at the end of its tail were so long that they poked up from under the boards.

"No, you don't!" she hollered. "You drop that baby!"

She grabbed a large, white stick that lay on the ground, dropped to her knees, and jabbed the creature's backside repeatedly, shouting at it to let the puppy go.

Mrs. Chamber wasn't sure what she was up against. From all she'd heard, the creature was vicious. But the adrenaline rushing through her body and her concern for the puppy were stronger than any rational thoughts of fear or caution.

The creature scurried out from under the porch and glared at her with red beady eyes. It hurried away from the house toward the woods. Mrs. Chamber expected such a ferocious beast to growl or bare its teeth, but it didn't. It simply slinked away, defeated by a determined woman with a stick.

Terrified, Mrs. Chamber set about looking under the porch for her puppy. She was afraid her heart might break if she saw one of her sweet pups mangled and lifeless. Holding her breath, she squinted into the dark shadows. Spotting a lump on the ground, she reached her hand toward it.

Mrs. Chamber gently pulled the small puppy out from under the porch and was relieved to feel it wiggle in her grip. When it turned its head toward her and licked her face, hot tears of relief rolled down her cheeks. She pulled the wiggly furball into her chest and hugged it.

Turning to look toward the woods, Mrs. Chamber wondered if the creature was watching her from the shadows. But sunlight shone brightly through the canopy of trees, leaving few places to hide. It seemed the would-be puppy thief was gone.

Upwards of three dozen men went out hunting for the creature in the coming days. Reported sightings came from across the county, with many of them centralized in the community of Statesville. While the beast was initially referred to as the Glutton, it soon became known as the Santer. Every newspaper in the area ran stories about the latest sightings. Some offered rewards up to $200 to anyone who captured the creature, dead or alive. But after a seasoned local policeman fired at the animal as it attacked a local dog, the Santer seemed to be unstoppable.

Locals reported hearing the beast howl in the forest—the sound of it likened to the wailing of a human baby. Others heard it scratching at doors and windows. It even disturbed a church service with all its scratching while the minister delivered his sermon.

While many reported seeing it, often running away with a pet or livestock in its mouth, no one seemed capable of trapping it or killing it. Hunters who found its tracks couldn't place the type of animal they belonged to. One local newspaper suggested that a prehistoric beast had emerged from the coal mines—a species extinct on the surface but somehow perfectly preserved deep in the Earth.

Whatever it was, it prowled and terrorized the area for decades. Newspapers reported new sightings as late as the 1930s. We may never know exactly what the creature was, but it wouldn't be dining on Mrs. Chamber's puppies as long as she was around to protect them.

Demon Dog of Valle Crucis

Valle Crucis, North Carolina
Summer 1860

The sun was about to set, and its impending departure worried 12-year-old Samuel to no end. He had strict rules.

He watched as the sun hit its halfway mark on the horizon and broke into a sprint, his fishing pole banging against his back. His mother was probably watching the sun's descent as well; she seemed to take pride in catching him breaking a rule. But he hadn't been late all summer. He didn't want to start now.

Samuel veered off the road to take his usual shortcut through a patch of woods that stretched behind St. John's Episcopal Church. He ran along this familiar path and grinned, knowing that he was going to make it. When he picked up the road again on the other side of the church, he'd be in eyesight of his mother, which was all that mattered.

Suddenly, his foot caught on something, and his body lurched forward. He skidded along the path on his belly, his arms and legs scraping in the dirt. Samuel fought back tears that were sparked by the pain. Picking himself up, he dusted off his shirt sleeves, only to notice several shredded holes with blood starting to soak through. His heart caught in his chest. Now, he was going to be late, and he was about to show up in bloody, torn clothes. His mother would be livid.

He glanced back to see what caused his fall. He knew this path well and had never tripped before. Wiping the dust from his eyes, he stared in disbelief. The dead body that lay in the path was bloody, torn, and missing an arm. It was impossible to tell who it had once been, but it was probably someone his family knew. In these parts, most people knew everyone else.

He picked up his fishing pole, not knowing what to do about the body. With a shudder, he hurried home. His mother's wrath over his tardiness and ruined clothes seemed less fearsome, given the mangled corpse on the path behind him.

* * *

In all, three bodies were found, mutilated and mangled. Everyone supposed it was some sort of bizarre animal attack.

As Samuel sat in church on Sunday, the minister preached about how he, himself, had seen the demon dog attack them and rip their bodies to shreds. Samuel wasn't sure this was true. Wouldn't a preacher stop to help those poor folks?

Samuel shrugged it off. He was just glad that his mother had forgotten about his torn-and-bloody clothes.

100 Years Later

Cameron kept his eyes on the road, and so did his friend Jeff in the passenger seat. The full moon lit up Highway 194 almost as well as the city streetlamps would back home. He'd been a student at Appalachian State for 3 years now, and the windy mountain turns still made for a white-knuckle drive. It didn't help that deer and other wildlife often darted into the road.

Cameron slowed down as he rounded the curve by the cemetery, and it was a good thing he did. Something leapt in front of his car out of the darkness.

Unable to stop fast enough, Cameron swerved to avoid it.

"Did you see that?" Cameron exclaimed.

"Yeah," replied Jeff. "It came from behind the tombstones."

Cameron moved the car to the side of the road. The young men turned in their seats, straining to see what it could have been.

A giant, dog-like creature lumbered slowly, pacing as if it were trying to discern what to do next. It was as big as either one of them, with dark fur that bristled.

"Do you see that?" Cameron asked again, this time with a whisper.

"No, and neither did you," Jeff replied, trying to convince himself that it wasn't really there.

But it was. It bared its yellow teeth in a growl. The beast's eyes glowed, an angry, threatening glare. It began to stalk toward them.

Cameron rammed his foot against the gas pedal, and the car sped off. Reaching up to 70 miles per hour, he took the sharp turns like a racecar driver.

A glance in his review mirror sent an icy fear through his veins. The demon dog was behind him. Not only was it following, but it was also keeping up with the car—and slowly gaining on them.

Cameron accelerated and flew across the bridge, where the creeks came together to form the cross that had inspired the town's name. But the beast did not follow him.

Slowing his car, he caught his breath.

"Dude, are you okay?" Jeff asked.

"No," Cameron answered, trying to keep his voice steady. His grip on the steering wheel remained tight to keep his hands from shaking.

"Let's stop somewhere," suggested Jeff. "There's a diner in Boone that's open all night."

Cameron nodded. He wasn't sure what he'd just sped away from. However, he felt certain that the encounter would haunt him for the rest of his life.

Bunny Man

Clifton, Virginia
October 31, 2023

Cara stood beside the road, shivering against the chilly October wind that gusted through the darkened tunnel in front of her. Above the concrete embankment that created the tunnel, the railroad tracks that ran through Fairfax County glimmered in the moonlight.

"This is where he strung the kids up," Ryan said, gesturing grandly toward the tunnel's opening. The flashlight in his hand cast long shadows across the blacktop road. "They were gutted like animals."

"Like the bunnies they found in the woods," Jenny added, giggling.

"How is that funny?" Sean asked.

"Sorry, I laugh when I'm nervous," Jenny replied, "or scared . . . or thinking I might get murdered by a psycho in a bunny suit."

"No one's getting murdered," Cara said, sounding more confident than she felt.

The four friends had grown up in Clifton and were aware of the gruesome legend associated with the bridge over Colchester Road. According to that legend, standing here so close to midnight on Halloween night was considered risky—if not deadly.

The legend claimed that, in 1904, a man, who was once housed in a local asylum, had escaped when a bus transporting residents to Lorton prison crashed. Local law enforcement scoured the area, but they were unable to locate him. Area residents began to find the bloodied bodies of bunnies strewn around the nearby woods. The man ate them to survive, leaving their disemboweled carcasses behind.

"Not long after the mutilated bunnies started showing up, a group of teens were hanging out here on Halloween night," Ryan continued, "just like we are now." He scanned his flashlight across the "No Trespassing" sign near the top of the tunnel. "They say the kids saw a bright flash of light before they were attacked—and as quickly as that, their lives were over."

Cara shivered at the thought, despite wondering how anyone could know about the flash of light if all the kids died.

Jenny giggled again.

"Still not funny," Sean said.

Ryan added, "They say if you're here at midnight on Halloween night, you'll end up just like those kids."

The story had frightened local children for decades. Cara knew that her own father had once stood in the shadow of the "Bunny Man Bridge," as it was commonly called, on a cold Halloween night 20 years before. Of course, she and her friends couldn't resist the possibility of seeing something paranormal on the creepiest night of the year.

"The first hole in this story is there are no records of an asylum ever existing in this area," Cara said. She was a history buff and had spent plenty of time researching this local legend. "Problem number two: There are zero reports of the murders ever happening."

The chime of an alarm emanated from Sean's pocket, causing everyone to jump. Jenny let out a high-pitched yelp. Sean pulled his phone from his pocket and thumbed his screen to stop the alarm he'd set for midnight. The four friends held their breaths, glancing around in the darkness, listening for signs that the Bunny Man might be approaching,

The chirp of crickets was the only sound they heard.

"See, it's just a stupid story," Sean said, shoving his phone back into his pocket.

"Well, there were a lot of reports in the papers about a man in a bunny suit threatening people with an axe back in October of 1970," Cara said.

The story of a strange man, who was said to be dressed in white with bunny ears on his head, ran in newspapers throughout the state and beyond. One evening, he reportedly threw an axe through the window of a parked car, where a young man and his girlfriend were sitting. The girl was cut by broken glass, and the terrified couple sped away.

Ten days later, the Bunny Man was seen again, this time by a night watchman who found a man, dressed in a bunny costume, using an axe to chop at the wooden supports on the front porch of a newly built home. The Bunny Man threatened to chop off the man's head before disappearing into the night.

The two incidents were so upsetting to local residents that some parents didn't allow their children to trick-or-treat that year. The police department in Washington, D.C., reported nearly two dozen calls from people claiming to see the "Bunny Man" on Halloween night.

Whether the story was true or not, the "Bunny Man" had haunted Fairfax County for decades—and would continue to do so as long as the legend persisted.

"We survived past midnight," Sean said. "Now I vote that we bounce."

A twig snapped somewhere in the distance. The friends' eyes widened as they looked from one another into the darkness.

"Yeah, let's not push our luck," Jenny agreed with a giggle.

As they began to depart along the paved path, they were temporarily blinded by a bright flash of light. Maybe it was just a car driving by on a nearby road. Or maybe it was the Bunny Man coming for them. Either way, the friends sprinted the rest of the way to their car, not willing to stick around to find out.

Green Hill Monster

Talihina, Oklahoma
October 1971

The group of football players pulled up to their favorite hangout spot: the dead-end turnoff at the end of Green Hill Road.

"Did you manage to ask Susan to the dance?" Edward asked Walter as the two boys got out of the truck.

Homecoming was only a week away.

Walter felt the sudden flush in his cheeks. Edward was tall and built like a wide receiver. Asking girls out came easy to him. It wasn't so easy for Walter, a burly offensive lineman.

"Yeah," said Walter. "She said yes."

Edward grinned. "Good, it'll be hip."

Together, they walked 300 yards to a clearing in the woods, where their friends had already started a campfire. One of their friends, Randy, tossed a log on the fire, and a spray of embers flew into the air, lighting up the available seats.

Walter found his favorite tree. It was set back a little from the campfire, but he was pretty sure it was the most comfortable spot. He situated his jacket as a cushion and settled himself on the ground. Leaning against the tree's large trunk, he took a deep breath. He was glad to be away from the noise of the pep fest they'd left behind.

After a while, he noticed Edward stand up and disappear beyond the trees—probably for a bathroom break.

In a matter of seconds, Edward crashed back through the trees. "Something tried to grab me," he exclaimed, and he continued running in the direction of the truck.

"What was that about?" asked their friend Elmer. He grabbed a lantern and shined it in the direction from which Edward had come.

There, in the woods, standing upright, a large hairy animal stared at the collection of teenagers with glowing red eyes.

Chaos erupted. Everyone scrambled away, back toward their cars. Walter grabbed his jacket and sprinted to his truck.

He found Edward already sitting in the cab. Walter shoved his keys into the ignition, started the vehicle, and peeled away from the scene. The other cars followed.

"The thing grabbed me from behind," Edward stammered, his voice unsteady.

Walter drove for a couple of miles and then pulled onto the side of the country road. He got out of his truck and halted the other cars for an impromptu meeting.

"We should tell someone," said Walter.

"A bunch of people are working on the homecoming float over in the Dressers' barn," noted Randy.

The caravan of cars went there to get help. When they arrived, Edward refused to get out of the truck. Walter studied his face. It was pale, as if fear had sucked all the color from it.

"You don't look good," he told Edward.

Edward stared back at him, his eyes empty.

Walter and the others found the group, including teachers, in the barn. They took turns explaining what had happened. In the presence of adults and more of their friends, the teenagers' courage was renewed. Walter wasn't sure whose idea it was, but he found himself in a longer caravan of cars, going back to the dead-end turnaround to look for signs of the creature.

As the string of cars parked, they were joined by two squad cars: one from the Highway Patrol and the other belonging to a county deputy. Walter's English teacher had Elmer and Edward repeat their stories.

The officers requested that the entire posse wait on the road, and they walked into the woods together. After a short time, they returned.

"Everyone should go," said the trooper.

"If you know what's good for you, you should get out of here," added the deputy.

"Did you see something?" asked the teacher.

"You should all go," the trooper repeated.

The assembled crowd didn't have any other choice but to get in their cars and leave. However, the next day, some of the group returned to explore the area in the daylight. Everyone at school had already begun talking about the Green Hill Monster.

In a nearby pasture, beyond a barbed wire fence, the boys spotted three animal carcasses rotting in the sun. The property owner was a friend of Randy's dad, so Randy quickly went to get him.

Several minutes later, a truck pulled up. Randy got out with the owner of the property. Together, they walked through the field to the dead deer.

The owner flipped one of the dead deer over. "There aren't any bullet holes," he said. "Their necks have been broken. Whatever did this used its bare hands."

Flintville Monster

Flintville, Tennessee
April 26, 1976

Jennie Robertson nestled her last dish into the rack to dry. As she rinsed out the sink and chased the last of the soap bubbles down the drain, she thought about how nice it was that her 4-year-old Gary could be trusted to play in the backyard by himself for a few minutes.

Her quiet moment of gratitude was pierced by a scream. She instantly knew it came from Gary. She rushed to the door and flung it open.

The moment she stepped outside, she was overwhelmed by a stench that filled the air. If a dead, decomposing rat and a skunk's foul spray could be combined to create the most obscene odor ever known, that was the smell that hung in her backyard.

Gary was sitting in his sandbox, frozen in place, screaming. Jennie followed his gaze and saw the source of his terror. A giant creature—about 8 feet tall with long hairy arms—was headed right for her child.

"Run!" she shrieked and sprinted toward her baby. She reached her son moments before the ape-like creature could. She then raced to the house and locked the door behind her.

Feeling much safer, she gathered the courage to peer out the window. With her son still grasped in her arms, she watched the tall black figure disappear into the woods that bordered her property. Terrified, she called the police.

Within an hour, her property turned into the headquarters of one of the strangest searches of the first responders' careers. Law enforcement officers arrived, weapons in hand. Hunters with shotguns and rifles volunteered to assist.

The posse set off into the woods with a resolve to kill the beast.

Inhuman screams pierced the forest air. At times, searchers were pelted with rocks. The monster managed to elude hunters and remained at bay. However, several footprints, measuring 16 inches long, were left behind as evidence. In addition, investigators found tufts of hair, as well as blood and mucus. The hair was sent to a lab, but results were inconclusive.

Beast of Okefenokee Swamp

Okefenokee National Wildlife Refuge, Georgia, April 2007

"Uncle Tony," Zach called. He walked up the sidewalk toward the Richard S. Bolt Visitor Center at the Okefenokee National Wildlife Refuge.

Tony stepped through the front door. His green uniform was perfectly pressed, as always. He gave a nod with the broad-brimmed hat that topped his head. He was the perfect picture of a park ranger.

"Howdy there, Zach," he replied, striding toward him. "Glad you could come along tonight."

"Thanks for letting me," Zach replied. He'd just gotten home from college for summer break and was glad to spend time with his uncle on a ride-along into the Okefenokee Swamp.

"Ranger Johnson was called to help with a fire, so it'll just be the two of us tonight," said Tony.

"There's a wildfire?"

"Yup, downed powerline over by Waycross," Tony replied. "Appears to be approaching the refuge. We've got most of the rangers on deck helping with that. But someone has to hold down the fort around here. Looks like I'm it."

Zach smiled. "I'm excited to tag along."

The pair walked to the airboat, stepped aboard, and started down the waterway. With 353,981 acres of marshy, peat-rich terrain to monitor, the airboat was the primary mode of transportation for the job. It was effective, efficient, and fun.

The sun dipped beyond the horizon, and the sky embraced the darkness of night. The duo traveled along the tree-lined water trail at a slow speed for 30 minutes.

Tony noticed a pair of kayakers, which was odd, given the time of night. He slowed the boat further as he approached the kayaks bobbing near one another in the light waves created by his approach.

"How ya doing, Bob? Jack?" Tony tipped his hat to each man as he said their names.

"Night got away from us," Jack said with an apologetic shrug.

"I know how that goes," Tony said. "But I have to shoo you out of here."

Jack nodded.

"I gotta tell ya: We've seen more gators today than we've ever seen in these waters before," Bob said, latching his fishing rod into place on the side of his kayak.

"We've seen a few more than usual ourselves," Tony replied. "I imagine it has something to do with the fire moving this way—has the wildlife all spooked. Probably pushing 'em toward the water for safety."

"That makes sense," Jack agreed. "There's a horde of them about 100 yards from here—and lots of other wildlife all bunched up in this one spot."

"I've never seen anything like it," Bob said. "Follow us, and we'll show you."

The pair kayaked slowly. Tony and Zach followed behind. It wasn't long before the bright light of the airboat lit up a section of water that was filled with gators.

"They're practically stacked on top of each other," Zach said in awe as he looked across the waterway.

The kayakers lingered just a few feet away from the mass—so close they almost could have reached out with a paddle and touched one. That was too close for Zach's comfort. He wished the kayakers would put a bit more space between them. Witnessing the incredible mass of alligators huddled together was amazing, but Zach didn't want to see them tear a man limb from limb. The thought made his pulse quicken.

Tony pulled a camera from his pack and took pictures to document the scene. For the most part, the alligators were calm, peacefully huddled together. An occasional bellow reverberated through Zach's body, as the creatures let out deep, rumbling growls.

Something broke the tranquility. The entire pod of gators broke into a flurry of flopping bodies. They scrambled in all directions, as if something had frightened them.

The pair of kayakers quickly paddled away from the chaos. Tony continued to take photos of the event, documenting as much as possible. The bright light of the airboat cast an eerie glow over the churning water.

"What made them freak out?" Zach wondered aloud.

A sudden movement pulled his attention to an area along the edge of the waterway. Something large, almost spider-like, stalked the shoreline. It was thin and spindly, with a body roughly the size of a full-grown bear. Thick black fur glistened over its long body, and the way the creature moved its round head reminded Zach of a monkey. It seemed to ponder the airboat and its occupants, its eyes sparkling in the boat's floodlight.

"What is that?" Zach yelled, pointing toward the beast. Goosebumps prickled his skin from head to toe as he watched the creature watching him back.

Tony's focus remained on the gators as he flashed photographs of them. Zach turned toward his uncle, hoping to get his attention. He sensed that the strange creature was somehow responsible for the sudden flurry in the water.

As he turned, Zach was blinded by the floodlight. He pushed his palms into his eyes, as if he could rub the blindness from them. When his eyes refocused, he quickly turned back to the shoreline. The odd creature was gone.

"Did you see that thing?" Zach asked, his voice quivering.

"What thing?" his uncle asked.

"That weird primate-bear thing. It moved like a spider, and it was watching us from the shore."

Tony cocked his head to one side and raised an eyebrow. Zach instantly regretted asking, as his uncle eyed him like he'd lost his mind.

"I didn't see any bear-spider-monkeys," he said. "Just a bunch of spooked gators."

Zach didn't reply. He just stared into the trees, feeling frightened and more than a little foolish.

"You okay?" Tony asked, putting a hand on Zach's back.

"Yeah, just . . . there was a lot going on for a few minutes."

"It's easy to get rattled out here at night," Tony said calmly.

Zach remained on edge the rest of the evening. He was relieved to get into his car a few hours later and even more relieved to drive away from the swamp. Yet he couldn't shake the fear that the beast might dart in front of his car. It never did, thankfully.

After doing some research, Zach discovered many stories about an unidentified beast in the Okefenokee Swamp. Witnesses described it as 6 to 7 feet long with the body of a bear covered in thick black fur, the head of a dog, and the tail of cat. Many reports involved the creature attacking cars, leaving deep scratches in the metal.

With so many acres of land, much of which is so desolate that no man has ever set foot on it, an elusive species could hide in the swamp—at least, that's what Zach concluded. He was thankful that the beast hadn't attacked the boat and that he wasn't the only one who'd ever seen it.

Rougarou

Terrebonne Parish, Louisiana
November 1, 1960

Thirteen-year-old Ricky stood in the forest, surveying his surroundings, his shotgun held carefully in his hands. It was late afternoon, and although he'd been hunting for 2 hours, he hadn't seen one rabbit. Maybe that was for the better. His mother had warned him not to hunt during All Saints Day or All Souls Day.

"You can't kill anything during the two days after Halloween," she told him firmly.

Both were important days of remembrance in the Catholic church, and hunting was strictly forbidden.

Ricky nodded his understanding, and his parents headed into town to pick up a few items at the store. The dust had barely settled on the gravel road leading away from their home when he had decided to go hunting anyway.

Hours later, he realized it was good that he wasn't coming home with fresh rabbits.

As he started making his way back, he was struck by an unsettling realization: The forest was unnaturally quiet—no trill of a bird or chirp from a cricket. Without a breeze, not even the leaves rustled. It was utterly and eerily silent.

The hairs on the back of Ricky's neck stood up as he surveyed his surroundings. He sensed that someone (or something!) was watching him. He wanted to hurry out of the woods, but his feet felt rooted to the ground. He was frozen by a fear that he couldn't understand.

"Stop being stupid," he scolded himself. He swallowed a lump in his throat and let out a long, deep breath.

As he entered a clearing, the blood reeds along the edge began to shake. The sound that might typically go unnoticed amid the normal forest noises was shockingly loud. Ricky stared into the reeds, straining to see what could be causing the movement. To his horror, a long finger with a pointed claw reached through the grass and a foot stepped out—or more like a paw.

Ricky's mouth opened, but no sound came out. Staring back at him was a 7-foot-tall creature with broad shoulders and a narrow lower extremity. Its thick, muscular frame was covered in dark, scraggly fur. It stood on two legs like a man but had a face that looked like a dog.

Ricky didn't raise his shotgun. He was facing a Rougarou, and he understood the repercussions of drawing the creature's blood. He turned and ran as fast as he could toward home.

Twigs snapped behind him as the beast gave chase. Ricky didn't dare turn around to look, but he knew the Rougarou was close because he could feel its hot breath against the back of his neck.

As he crashed through the brush, into the clearing that encircled his family's home, he could no longer hear the creature coming after him. He turned in time to see a blur of movement retreat into the woods. The chase was over.

Ricky looked down at his feet and saw that he only had one boot on. His other must have come off while he ran. He hurried to the house and stumbled into the kitchen. His lungs and legs burned from the effort. He dropped into a chair and tried to catch his breath.

His mother stood at the counter, emptying a small bag of groceries.

"What in the Sam Hill . . ." she began. She looked up and saw Ricky's face, drained of blood and sheet white. She eyed the shotgun he'd set on the table in front of himself. "You saw it," she said, her voice a whisper.

Ricky nodded.

"You didn't shoot it, did you?" Her eyes widened with fear.

"No, I knew not to."

His family had lived in Terrebonne Parish for generations. He'd heard the stories of the Rougarou and knew that if you shot one, the curse that gripped it would soon grip you. The creature actually wanted you to take aim and fire, so it could pass the curse on to you.

"That's good," his mother nodded. Her shoulders relaxed. "You go on and put that gun up. You can't shoot anything for nine days. If you do, it'll come back and do everything it can to lay its curse on you." She looked at the shotgun in front of him, then pointed to the rack on the wall.

Ricky complied, setting the gun on the rack where he'd found it earlier that afternoon. "I lost my boot," Ricky said.

His mother looked at his stocking-covered foot. His white sock was caked in mud, and a bit of blood had seeped through it.

"You ran clean out of your boot, did ya?" She smiled at Ricky. "Your father will go out and find it for you tomorrow. We'll give things a little time to settle first."

Ricky nodded. He wondered if the Rougarou was trying to get him to shoot it or if it was chasing him away from trouble, knowing that he was hunting on a holy day of obligation. Either way, the boy had no intention of disobeying his parents or breaking the traditions of his faith again—or venturing into those woods alone.

Ricky's gun sat on that rack for nearly a year before he picked it up again.

Lake Worth Monster/Goatman

Greer Island, Texas
July 9, 1969

John pulled the car to the side of the road. Lots of couples parked here, in the clearing under the trees—and they all did so for the same reason that the teens in the car were there now. The summer chorus of cicadas and katydids sang their night songs.

John clicked on the radio, and the Beatles filled the air.

"It's so hot," Mary said, leaning her head out the window.

"It's July," said John. "Of course, it's hot."

"It's too hot to make out," Kathryn said.

"What? It's never too hot to make out," Michael replied, wrapping his arm around her.

A loud *kerchunk* and then a *thump* shook the roof of the car. The girls screamed.

"What was that?" Kathryn yelled.

"It sounds like something fell on the car," replied John.

"But what?" asked Mary. "A raccoon?"

"It was probably a monster," Michael said with a maniacal laugh.

Kathryn punched his arm in response. "Stop it. Don't make fun."

Suddenly, a creature stood up next to the passenger side of the car, right beside Mary. It reached its arm through the open window and grabbed her arm.

Her piercing scream startled the creature, and it retracted its hand.

John started the car, and the engine revved to life. The vehicle roared away, leaving a trail of dust behind it.

The passengers in the backseat watched out the rear window, trying to see what they were escaping from.

"What was it?" asked Kathryn.

"I don't know," Mary said, shaking. "It was tall, and it had a long, furry neck. Its face looked like a goat." She massaged her arm, where the creature had grabbed her. "Its long claws grabbed me."

John put his arm around her and pulled her close while he drove. His brow furrowed. "We need to call the police."

* * *

The police dispatcher hung up the phone. He'd been getting similar calls for the last two months about a half-goat/half-man creature that was terrorizing residents. The other calls could be laughed off as pranks, but this time was different. This time, the Goatman had attacked a car full of teenagers.

He picked up the radio. "You're not going to believe this one, but I think we need to check it out."

* * *

The officer ran his hand along the deep scratch in the passenger-side door. It was at least 18 inches long.

"It jumped out of the trees and landed on top of the car," said John.

"We all heard it," Michael added.

"It was terrifying," said Kathryn.

"And it grabbed me," added Mary, her voice barely a whisper.

"Okay, we will see what we can find," promised the officer.

The department had been joking about these sightings for weeks, but it was time to open an investigation.

July 10, 1969

By the next day, men had arrived by the truckload, armed with guns and fortified by beer. It was a posse party, the likes of which the town had never seen. A few dozen people were gathered near Greer Island, not far from where the beast had attacked a woman the day before, near the junkyard dumping ground.

"Look," shouted a man, pointing at the cliff. "There it is!"

Before anyone had time to aim a weapon, the monster gave a pitiful cry. It sounded as if someone was causing it great pain.

It picked up an old tire and threw it 500 feet.

Panicked screams spread throughout the group, and everyone ran away in fear—even the deputies who had been called in to keep the peace.

Monster Creatures of the Water

White River Monster

Newport, Arkansas
July 1937

"Mr. Bateman, it was over here."

Bramlett Bateman followed his farmhand through the trees to the edge of the river. The farmhand, along with a few others, had reported seeing a creature in the water earlier that morning. Bramlett couldn't wait to see the beast for himself.

As they reached the final stretch of trees, the farmhand held a finger to his lips, indicating for Bramlett to be quiet.

Bramlett frowned. He was usually the one giving orders. It didn't sit well with him that he was being directed to do anything by anyone. But he obliged, only because a rare opportunity was before him.

He'd heard rumors of the elusive beast, dating back to childhood. A newspaper article he'd read as a boy talked about loggers who had seen the sea creature while transporting cedar trees along the White River. Ever since, he'd wanted to see it for himself. He hoped today would be the day that childhood wish became reality.

The local fishermen complained that something was stealing their catches. If this monster were on his property, he planned to take control and do something about it. He took off his hat and patted his sweaty forehead with a handkerchief.

The farmhand pulled back some brush, so Bramlett could step through. The grin that stretched across the man's face told Bramlett all that he needed to know: The creature was still there.

Nevertheless, Bramlett could barely believe his own eyes. The creature was long and gray. Its skin glistened in the hot summer sun as it lumbered about in the eddy. It seemed to be having a grand old time, flopping around in the slow current.

Bramlett tried to judge its size, but that was difficult to do while it sat mostly underwater. It was big—and no doubt needed a lot of the local fish to keep its belly full. Bramlett wished he'd brought his pistol. From the riverbank, he would have had a perfect shot at it.

A plan began to percolate in his mind. He could single-handedly save the town from this strange beast—by blasting the beast to kingdom come. A few well-laid sticks of dynamite would do the trick.

Unfortunately, that plan never got off the ground. Bramlett was unable to secure a permit to blow up the river where the creature had been spotted. Further efforts to stretch a net across the river were thwarted by logistical issues—the river was nearly 75 feet wide at that point.

Bramlett told anyone who would listen about the monstrous beast, describing it as wide as a car and as long as three. Men staked out the area with guns, but the beast evaded sight, making Bramlett wish, yet again, he'd had a pistol with him that first day.

By July 13, news of the creature had spread across the country, and visitors flocked to the area. A fence was erected, and sightseers were charged 25¢ for a chance to spot the beast.

The Chamber of Commerce hired a professional diver. Charles B. Brown donned a helmet and a rubber suit. Carrying an 8-foot harpoon, he was lowered 60 feet to the river's bottom. He came up empty-handed.

Sightings continued through the decades. Some witnesses compared its size to a train car. Still others were convinced it was much smaller. Some said the beast had a bone protruding from its head like a horn.

In July 1971, strange three-toed footprints—more than a foot long—were found on an island near crushed vegetation. It was as if something had come out of the water to take a nap.

In 1973, Arkansas state lawmakers designated a White River Monster Refuge from Newport to Possum Grape. It is now illegal to hunt, kill, or otherwise harm a water monster along that stretch of the White River.

St. Augustine Sea Monster

St. Augustine, Florida November 30, 1896

Herbert Coles ran across the sand and jumped as high as he could, landing hard with both feet. "Watch this!" he shouted to his older friend, 12-year-old Dunham Coretter. He did it again.

Dunham rolled his eyes at his 10-year-old friend. "That's neat," he said, humoring him. "But you're going to get sand in your shoes."

"Nah," said Herbert, "and anyways, it's okay. I'll just dump it out like I always do."

The boys continued walking.

"Look up there!" Herbert pointed to a blob-type mass ahead on the beach.

"Whoa," gasped Dunham. "C'mon, let's go."

Together, they ran toward the strange mass.

"Do you think it's a whale?" Herbert asked. "I've always wanted to see a whale."

"Maybe," Dunham replied. He slowed to a walk. "It's November, so I guess it could be. My dad says whales come to Florida during winter."

Their walk slowed, as if they suddenly weren't sure they wanted to see the creature.

"It's just a big blob of goo," Herbert said.

"Well, it used to be something," said Dunham. "But it got tossed around in the ocean and then washed up here. Half of it is even buried in the sand—it's giant."

"It gives me the willies," Herbert said with a shiver.

Dunham nodded. "We should go tell someone about it."

The boys rode their bicycles back to town and found the most serious person they could think of: the town's physician, Dr. DeWitt Webb.

The next day, Dr. Webb visited the washed-up sea creature. He noted that the body was pear-shaped, about 18 feet long and 7 feet wide. It had four stumps, either for arms or tentacles, and it indeed seemed to be a gray glob of goo.

Aware of the discovery's significance, Dr. Webb had the creature photographed. He concluded that it was a giant octopus of sorts and reached out to a professor at Yale, Addison E. Verrill.

Dr. Webb also took a sample of tissue from the creature and sent it, along with the photographs, to the Smithsonian, where William Healy Dall, the museum's curator, logged it. (It remains there to this day.)

In 1897, Professor Verrill announced the discovery in the newspapers, naming the newly found creature an *octopus giganteus*. He later revised his conclusion that the mass was part of a whale. For decades, scientists debated the classification of the strange water creature. In 2004, DNA tests from the Smithsonian sample confirmed that it was a whale. But despite the definitive proof, some still believe that in 1896, a legendary kraken-octopus washed up onshore.

Lizard Man of Scape Ore Swamp

Bishopville, South Carolina Summer 1988

Chris Davis was exhausted and glad to be heading home after a long shift at a fast-food restaurant. Keeping his eyes on the road, the 17-year-old turned up the volume on the radio. There was nothing like driving with the windows down and the radio blaring to reset his energy level.

Suddenly, he felt his car lurch. Trying not to panic, he put on his turn signal—not that he needed it on this country road, near the edge of Scape Ore Swamp. Chris hadn't seen another vehicle for miles, and at this time of night, he wasn't likely to see one anytime soon.

Slowly, he pulled the car to the side of the road. "Great," he mumbled, "just great."

He climbed out, looked at the flat tire with a sigh, then went to the trunk and grabbed the tire jack. Fishing the spare tire out of its compartment, he wondered if his dad had jinxed him by making him learn how to change a flat.

Chris worked for several minutes, his senses tuning in to the sounds of the night. Crickets and frogs chirped happily in the nearby swamp. A cloud of mosquitoes buzzed, held at bay by the bug spray that also happened to be in the trunk.

With the tire changed, Chris put everything back into the trunk. His ears tuned to a different sound: Footsteps. Running.

Who would be running along the road at this time of night?

He turned and looked down the dark highway—and saw a strange creature charging toward him. Whatever it was, it was at least 7 feet tall and had strange lizard feet.

Adrenaline shot through his veins and spurred him to action. Chris slammed the trunk closed and ran to the driver's seat. Safely inside, he started the car and revved the engine. The monster peered into the window, and Chris stared into its red eyes. Its skin was scaly and green.

The creature grabbed at the side mirror. Using it as a step, it climbed onto the roof of the car, and Chris saw that its webbed feet had three toes. As the mirror crashed to the ground, Chris hoped that he'd secured the spare tire correctly. He took off with a swerve, shaking the monster off his car and into the road behind him.

After a few days, Chris was convinced to report the incident. Not quite sure what to think of his tale, Sheriff Liston Truesdale administered a polygraph test, which Chris passed. Not long after that, deputies found large, three-toed footprints in the swamp, which were preserved with plaster casts.

* * *

In the weeks that followed Chris Davis's harrowing experience, a local radio station offered a $1 million reward for the capture of this Lizard Man. While the reward was never claimed, Chris wasn't the only one who saw the creature.

In 2015, at least three sightings were reported: one from a woman who claimed to have photographed the creature on her mobile phone, another from a man who said he captured video of the creature but never shared it for fear that everyone would think he'd lost his mind. The third report came from a man named Jim Wilson, who encountered it while driving along Highway 34. As he approached Scape Ore Bridge, something scrambled over the side rail and scurried across the road in front of him. According to Jim, it was tall and had scales. It looked like an alligator but with long legs. He also managed to photograph the creature as it crossed the bridge and entered the swamp.

With so many images of the creature available online, one might think the world would decide, "It really does exist!" Unfortunately, even with such evidence, it's too easy to rationalize away the possibility that a lizard man could be hunting around Scape Ore Swamp. Perhaps the only way people will ever believe in monsters is to see them for themselves.

"Normie" the Lake Norman Monster

Lake Norman, North Carolina Summer 2021

Heather dipped her paddle into the lake and pushed her kayak through the still water. She'd been kayaking on Lake Norman since she was a little girl. Her grandparents had owned a home along the shoreline that was passed down to Heather's parents. Heather made the most of the warm summer months, often spending weekends there with her own daughter.

Heather had always been fascinated by the history of the lake. Her grandmother shared fond memories of attending the old summer camp that now sat on the bottom of the reservoir floor. Her grandfather recalled watching the water rise after the Duke Power Company bought the land and began flooding the area. Over the span of 2 years, the water swallowed homes, old plantations, highways, and even the old bridge that once carried traffic across the river. Even a Revolutionary-War-era battlefield now rested far below the surface. Heather found it wild to think that she was paddling in space that once made up the sky for people who had lived in the valley below.

This morning, as her paddle slipped in and out of the lake, she enjoyed the quiet symphony of nature beginning a new day. Birds chirped in the oaks and willows along the shoreline. Water lapped softly against the side of her kayak. Breathing in fresh air, Heather admired the bright orange of the horizon as the sun began to wake for the day.

The serenity was disrupted when something rose out of the water just a foot in front of her kayak. It appeared to be a head with a gray snout. Water streamed from it as it rose at least 3 feet above the water.

Heather stopped paddling and let her kayak float alongside the odd creature.

A spray of water erupted from the snout, raining down on her. She held her breath as the cold water drenched her clothes. Although the creature didn't seem interested in hurting her, a thought occurred to her that perhaps it just hadn't noticed her. She watched quietly, her wet hair clinging to her cheeks, as the creature lowered itself quietly back into the water.

Heather looked into the lake, wondering if she might see the creature swimming beneath her. She silently hoped its glowing eyes would illuminate the water—as others had reported. But there was nothing to see. The only remnants of the odd scene were ripples of water, expanding outward from where the creature had slipped beneath the surface.

Returning her paddle to the water, she resumed her journey, a smile spreading across her lips. She knew the stories of Normie, the lake monster reported by so many over the past 60 years, but she'd never seen it before.

Many homeowners and visitors to Lake Norman had reported sighting it. Pictures of its long body, of something peaking just above the surface, circulated across the internet.

Perhaps her favorite story about Normie came from a scuba diver, who went exploring in the submerged buildings at the bottom of the lake. He planned to enter a home on the reservoir floor through a hole in its side. But as he peered into it, he was startled by how dark it was, compared to how clear everything looked outside the home. He shone his diving light inside and observed the biggest fish he'd ever seen. It was at least 8 feet long and 3 feet wide. He did not join that monstrous fish inside the house.

What Heather saw didn't appear to be a large fish, though. What kind of fish had a long neck and sprayed water from its snout? But that was the fun thing about the sea monster that lived in Lake Norman: There were so many variations in the description that it left one wondering if there might be a variety of mysterious creatures swimming through the ruins that sit silently below.

Is Normie a catfish of epic proportions? Is it a serpent-like creature, measuring 50 feet long, with fins and scales and a head that resembles a horse's? Whatever it might be, one thing is certain: Normie is a legend that's not going away anytime soon.

Lake Herrington Monster

Herrington Lake, Kentucky August 1972

Dr. Lawrence S. Thompson, a college professor, stood at the water's edge and stared across the lake, as he did almost every morning while at his summer home on Herrington Lake. A man of routine, his days began with a walk, during which he'd study the shoreline and observe nature. However, this day was different. Today, he was looking for something.

A few days earlier, he'd walked to Wells Landing. At the Chenault Bridge, he'd seen an anomaly in the water—something unexpected. It had a snout and a hump of some kind in the middle of its body. A tail, like that of an alligator, trailed 15 feet behind the creature as it glided through the water.

Dr. Thompson desperately wanted to know what it was, although he tried not to get too excited that he'd seen some lifeform that hadn't yet been discovered. He looked for it now, as he had every morning since he first saw it.

Winter 1973

The reporter trudged up the front steps of the house. A writer for the *Kentucky Kernel,* she'd been sent to interview an eccentric professor from the University of Kentucky. She knocked on the door, and Professor Thompson opened it as if he'd been waiting on the other side for exactly this moment.

As he led her into the den, the reporter marveled at the floor-to-ceiling bookshelves. "You have a lot of books," she said in awe.

"This is only a small portion of them," said the professor. "I also have books in the basement and the garage. I developed my own card catalog system to keep them straight."

"That's impressive."

"It's a necessity," the professor explained. "If I'm going to have all of these books, I need to be able to find the one I want, when I want it."

"Yes, I can understand that." The writer nodded. "You have them in the garage too?"

"Oh, yes," said the professor. "Along with the family of possums that live in there."

The reporter raised an eyebrow but didn't say anything. She sat in the seat that the professor offered and took out her notebook. She quickly scribbled a few notes.

She waited until the professor settled behind his desk and lit up the end of a cigar. Her nose wrinkled at the stench, as smoke filled the air. "Why don't you tell me about what you saw?"

"Did you know I have the oldest man-made thing in Lexington?" he asked.

"Really?" she said. "What would that be?"

"I have an Egyptian papyrus that dates back to about 1500 B.C."

"Really?" she said again, not sure how that fit in with why she was there.

"Have you always been interested in monsters and creatures?" she asked, trying to steer the conversation to the purpose for her visit.

"Oh, yes, I am quite interested in humanity's dealings with monsters and mythical beasts throughout time." He went to his card catalog drawers. "Would you like to see some books on the subject?"

"No, sir, I don't think that will be necessary. Why don't we start with you telling me what you saw? You mentioned that it was a monster with a snout and a long tail, swimming through the water?"

"Yes! You know, though," he said, puffing on his cigar thoughtfully. "When the Europeans arrived, they thought the alligators were monsters, simply because they'd never seen them before. I suppose it could have been an alligator."

"An alligator?" she asked.

"Don't you remember? There was a circus train that crashed near the lake a few years ago. It could have escaped and lived in the caves along the gorge. It'd surely be too cold for you and me, but an alligator might be able to survive."

The reporter was quiet, trying to imagine an alligator would survive a Kentucky blizzard.

"It could have been a giant catfish," the professor volunteered. "They've been known to grow up to 12 feet." He took another puff. "It could have gone up the Mississippi, Ohio, Kentucky, and Dix rivers and gotten trapped when the dam was built."

The reporter scribbled in her notebook.

"Appearances may be deceptive when our brains try to make sense of something unfamiliar. In the 1850s, several people on a boat in the ocean were entirely convinced that a sea monster was following them." He paused, as if waiting for her undivided attention.

The reporter stopped scribbling and looked up.

"It turned out to be a log that was caught on the ship's cable. The boat was just dragging it along."

"Some say you are mistaken," the reporter suggested. She flipped back in her notebook. "For example, Roy Riley, the owner of the Kamp Kennedy dock, thinks you were drinking the wrong kind of whiskey and suggested this is all a big hoax."

The professor sighed. "This is not a joke. I have always been interested in monsters, and I'm convinced they do exist, some since the dawn of time."

The reporter scribbled, making sure to get his exact words recorded.

"We've found crude rock drawings of monsters by prehistoric men from 1,500 to 2,500 years ago."

"Have you seen the creature since?" the reporter asked.

"No," said the professor. "I suspect it prefers to keep to itself, living in the depths of Lake Harrington."

The reporter flipped her notebook closed. "Thank you for your time, professor. Will you call me if you think of anything else you'd like to add?"

He walked with her to the door. "This I know," he said. "I will keep trying to prove it to myself. But the question is in your mind. Does it exist?"

As the reporter drove away, she tried to make sense of the unusual interview. Ultimately, she agreed with him: He had left the question in her own mind.

Does the Lake Herrington monster really exist? She wasn't any closer to knowing the truth.

Bibliography

LITTLE GRAY MEN *(Kelly/Hopkinsville, KY)*

Carey, Liz. "Legend of 'Little Green Men' Invading Kelly, Kentucky, Continues." *The Daily Yonder* (thedailyyounder.com). October 22, 2021.

"The Kelly-Hopkinsville Encounter | Documentary." Fire of Learning (youtube.com). October 20, 2022.

Janssen, Volker. "How the 'Little Green Men' Phenomenon Began on a Kentucky Farm." History.com (history.com). September 14, 2023.

Moore, Erick. "Steven Spielberg, Some Green Men, and Hopkinsville." *Kentucky for Kentucky* (kyforky.com). August 22, 2015.

MOON MAN *(Killgore Hills, MS)*

"Bonus | The Moon Man of Kilgore Hills." Patreon (patreon.com). April 29, 2023.

Burleson, Brook Bullock. "Legend or Legendary: The Moon Man of Kilgore Hills." *Daily Journal* (djournal.com). July 24, 2022.

SNALLYGASTER *(Preston County, WV)*

Charles, Ken and Royal Mallory, Colt Straub, and Duke Straub. Producers: Bluemke, Jay and Carlos Castellanos. "Snallygaster of Preston County" *Mountain Monsters* (Season 1: Episode 16). June 20, 2014.

Dogwood Staff. "The Snallygaster & Bunny Man: 4 of Virginia's creepiest cryptids." Dogwood (vadogwood.com). May 30, 2024.

Stein, Charles F. Jr. "Add Snallygaster." *The Evening Sun*. September 7, 1951.

Tabler, Dave. "It's the Snallygaster." Appalachian History (appalacianhistory.net). November 5, 2018.

MOTHMAN *(Clendenin and Point Pleasant, WV)*

Alexander, Kathy. "The Mothman of West Virginia." Legends of America (legendsofamerica.com). Updated March 2023.

Klein, Shayla. "The Legend of Mothman." Paranormal W.VA.12 WBoy (wboy.com). November 12, 2021.

Mallow, Gwen. "An Ode to a Hometown Creature: Mothman of Point Pleasant, West Virginia." Smithsonian Center for Folklife & Cultural Heritage (folklife.si.edu). June 7, 2021.

"Mothman." History.com (history.com). Accessed on September 22, 2024.

Sibray, David. "Did legendary Mothman first appear near Elk River Trail?" West Virginia Explorer (wvexplorer.com). July 19, 2022.

Tarbett Hardiman, Jean. "Silver Bridge collapse: 40 years later." Skyscraper City (skyscrapercity .com). December 14, 2007.

Turner, Mark. "Couples See Man-Sized Bird... Creature...Something!" *Point Pleasant Register.* November 16, 1966.

Zurcher, Neil. "The Silver Bridge Collapse: An Excerpt from *Ten Ohio Disasters.*" Gray & Company Publishers (grayco.com). Accessed on September 22, 2024.

HOUSTON BATMAN *(Houston, TX)*

No author. "'Houston Batman' remains mystery decades after reported encounter." ABC 13 (abc13.com). June 17, 2018.

Rice, Laura. "The mysterious sightings of the Houston Batman." Texas Public Radio (tpr.org). October 27, 2023.

Staff writer. "Eerie Batman Report Stumps Cops." *The Springfield News-Leader.* June 19, 1953.

FLYING MONSTER OF MYRTLE BEACH *(Myrtle Beach, SC)*

Martinez, Ava. "South Carolina Cryptids: From Lizard Man to Boo Hags." Hangar 1 Publishing (hangar1publishing.com). Accessed on October 5, 2024.

No author. "Horrifying Flying Cryptid Encounter–Northeast South Carolina." Phantoms & Monsters: Pulse of the Paranormal (phantoms and monsters.com). March 1, 2017

ALABAMA WHITE THANG *(Hurricane Mountain, AL)*

Gosset, Peter J. "'The White Thang' Animal or Ghost?" Free State of Winston (freestateofwinston .org). Accessed on August 7, 2024.

McNamara, Samantha. "Legendary 'Alabama White Thang' and Courtland's 'Slough Thing': Enigmas of Lawrence." *The Moulton Advertiser* (moultonadvertiser.com). October 11, 2023.

Murphy, Elias. "Cryptids of the South: The White Thang of Alabama." *East Tennessean* (easttennessean.com). January 18, 2024.

No author. "Alabama's 'most mythical creature' is one you've probably not heard of." AL.com (al.com). March 25, 2019.

"Classic Appalachian Cryptid Tales Collection." Spooky Appalachia (youtube.com). July 26, 2024.

BOGGY BAYOU BIGFOOT *(Cotton Island, LA)*

Baty, Jann. "Boggy Bayou 'Bighoax'?" *The Town Talk*. August 28, 2000.

Burdeau, Cain. "Bigfoot of the Boggy Bayou lays down tracks." *The Anniston Star.* September 17, 2000.

Griffin, Andrew. "Bigfoot: real or hoax?" *The Town Talk*. August 30, 2000.

SKUNK APE *(The Everglades, FL)*

Cosgrove, John (director). *Unsolved Mysteries* (Season 10: Episode 5). May 22, 1998.

"Hunting for the elusive Florida Skunk Ape." ABC7 SWFL (YouTube.com). August 22, 2019.

Murphy, Elias. "The Skunk Ape of the Florida Everglades." *ET Online* (easttennessean.com). March 20, 2024.

No author. "Sniffing out the Skunk Ape." *Tampa Bay Times*. November 2, 1997.

Runnells, Charles. "Attraction traps tourists, but no Skunk Apes." *News Press*. September 26, 2007.

Talcott, Anthony. "Florida 'Skunk Ape' reported across the state. Here's where it's been sighted." WKMG 6 (clikcorlando.com). March 3, 2024.

CHATAWA MONSTER *(Chatawa, MS)*

Grayson, Walt. "Focused on Mississippi: Chatawa Monster." WJTV (wjtv.com). July 17, 2020.

"Paranormal Mississippi Case File #5: The Chatawa Monster: Mississippi's Big Foot." Library Guides Hinds Community College (libguides.hindscc.edu). Accessed on September 8, 2024.

"Past, present and future of St. Mary of the Pines." School Sisters of Notre Dame: Century Pacific Provence (ssndcentralpacific.org). Accessed on September 8, 2024.

GEORGIA WEREWOLF *(Woodland, GA)*

"Emily Isabella Burt – Georgia Werewolf." Dixie After Dark (YouTube.com). October 22, 2023.

Hartwell, John. "Emily Isabella Burt, the Georgia Werewolf." Civil War Talk (civilwartalk.com). June 27, 2022.

No author. "Grave of the Georgia Werewolf." Roadtrippers (roadtrippers.com). Accessed on September 2, 2024.

WILD WOLF WOMAN *(Mobile, AL)*

Deal, Marissa. "Port City Legends." *Mobile Bay* (mobilebaymag.com). October 31, 2023.

No author. "The Wolf-Woman of Mobile Alabama." Spooky Appalachia (spookyappalachia.com). April 9, 2024.

"Original drawing of legendary Wolf Woman of Mobile discovered in archives." AL.com (AL.com). October 20, 2015.

FOUKE MONSTER OF BOGGY CREEK *(Fouke, AR)*

Mobley, Andrew. "'That's no deer': Fouke Monster legend haunts swamplands of southwest

Arkansas with new alleged evidence." *KATV News* (katv.com). October 23, 2023.

Powell, Jim. "Hairy 'monster' hunted in Fouke sector." *Texarkana Gazette* (texarkanagazette .com). May 3, 1971 rerun June 14, 2019.

Rice, Joe David. "Arkansas Backstories: Fouke Monster." *About You Magazine* (aymag.com). September 26, 2019.

Robinson, Kat. "Finding the Fouke Monster in Southwest Arkansas." Tie Dye Travels (tiedyetravels.com). March 10, 2016.

Thompson, Amy Michelle. "Fouke Monster." Encyclopedia of Arkansas (encyclopediaofarkansas.net). June 16, 2023.

GLUTTON / SANTER *(Statesville, NC)*

Menke, Aaron. "Lore Legends: North Carolina Monsters." Lore Podcast (YouTube.com). May 14, 2023.

No author. "Mysterious 'Santer' Wanders Streets of Statesville." Downtown Statesville (downtownstatesville.com). April 25, 2024.

Staff writer. "The 'Antelope' or 'Glutton'— A New Sensation Among the Colored People." *The Lenoir Topic*. September 4, 1890.

DEMON DOG OF VALLE CRUCIS *(Valle Crucis, NC)*

Kinkaid, Ezekiel. "The Demon Dog of Valle Crucis, North Carolina an Urban Legend." Puzzle Box Horror (puzzleboxhorror.com). June 26, 2020.

No author. "The Demon Dog of Valle Crucis." Wordpress.com (ekim2012.wordpress.com). October 14, 2012.

No author. "The Demon Dog of Valle Crucis," North Carolina Ghosts (NorthCarolinaGhosts.com). Accessed on August 28, 2024.

"The Demon Dog of Valle Crucis, North Carolina." Real Appalachia (youtube.com). October 22, 2021.

BUNNY MAN *(Clifton, VA)*

Griffin, James. "Doctors say Bunny Man's mind is hopping." *The Washington Daily News*. November 11, 1970.

Schweitzer, Ally. "The True Story of the Bunnyman, Northern Virginia's Most Gruesome Urban Legend." WAMU 88.5 (wamu.org). October 31, 2017.

Staff writer. "Where Did the Bunny Man Go?" *The Berkeley Gazette*. Dec. 9, 1970.

GREEN HILL MONSTER *(Talihina, OK)*

Hill, Randy. "The Green Hill Monster." Randy Hill (youtube.com). March 25, 2024.

No author. "The Green Hill Monster." *Sasquatch Chronicles Blog* (sasquatchchronicles.com). Accessed on September 22, 2024.

No author. "Report #2909." The Bigfoot Field Researchers Organization (bfro.net). July 27, 2001.

FLINTVILLE MONSTER *(Flintville, TN)*

Floyd, Randall E. "The Flintville Monster, Tennessee 1997." *The Augusta Georgia Chronicle* (bigfootencounters.com). April 6, 1997.

Romano, Anthony. "Terror in Tennessee: The Flintville Monster's Reign of Terror." Hangar 1 Publishing (hangar1publishing.com). Accessed on September 21, 2024.

BEAST OF OKEFENOKEE SWAMP
(Okefenokee National Wildlife Refuge, GA)

Author Unknown. "Unknown 'Swamp Creature' Seen in the Okefenokee National Wildlife Refuge." *Journal News* (journalnews.com). April 20, 2022.

No author. "Okefenokee Swamp." Create-A-Cryptid Wiki (createacriptid.fandom.com) Accessed on September 22, 2024.

No author. "Georgia's Own Swamp Thing." Georgia Public Broadcasting (GBP.org). Accessed on September 22, 2024.

ROUGAROU *(Terrebonne Parish, LA)*

LeCompte, Lillian. "Rougarou: The Swamp Werewolf." Terrebonne Parish Library (mytpl.org). Accessed on September 28, 2024.

Moser, Heather (writer). Breedlove, Seth (director). "Skinwalker: The Howl of the Rougarou." September 1, 2021.

Renfro, Alisha. "Save the Swamp: But, Beware of the 'Rougarou.'" National Wildlife Federation (blog.nwf.org). October 19, 2019.

LAKE WORTH MONSTER / GOATMAN
(Greer Island, TX)

Hodge, Larry D. "The Lake Worth Monster." Texas Parks & Wildlife (tpwmagazine.com). Accessed on September 28, 2024.

Scudder, Charles. "Greer Island's Goatman." *The Dallas Morning News* (res.dallasnews.com). Accessed on September 28, 2024.

Vaughn, Chris. "Mystery Still Engulfs Lake Worth Monster." 5NBCDFW (nbcdfw.com). August 6, 2009.

WHITE RIVER MONSTER *(Newport, AR)*

Busbee, Jay. "Beware the White River Monster." Flashlight & A Biscuit (jaybusbee.substack.com). June 18, 2022.

Cox, Dale. "A River Monster in Arkansas? The White River Monster–Newport and Jacksonport, Arkansas." Explore Southern History.com (exploresouthernhistory.com). Accessed on September 2, 2024.

Shaw, Kate. "Episode 153: The White River Monster." *Strange Animals Podcast* (strangeanimalspodcast.blubrry.net). January 6, 2020.

ST. AUGUSTINE SEA MONSTER *(St. Augustine, FL)*

Covert, Robert. "St. Augustine Sea Monster?" St. Augustine Historical Society (staughs.com). Accessed on September 21, 2024.

Markey, Mary. "The Saint Augustine Monster." Smithsonian Institution Archives (siarchives .si.edu). August 18, 2010.

LIZARD MAN OF SCAPE ORE SWAMP *(Bishopville, SC)*

Jackson, Gavin and A T Shire. "The Lizard Man of Bishopville | South of Spooky." South Carolina ETV (scetv.org). October 24, 2022.

Moore, Thad. "Bishopville's journey to reclaim a South Carolina monster." Post and Courier (postandcourier.com). Accessed on September 21, 2024.

Whetsel, Gee. "The Lizard Man of Scape Ore Swamp." The City of Bishopville (cityofbishopvillesc.com). Accessed on September 14, 2024.

dailymail.co.uk/news/article-3188604/Is-South-Carolina-s-Lizard-Man-New-images-claim-mythic-swamp-monster-prankster-lizard-costume.html

"NORMIE" THE LAKE MONSTER

(Lake Norman, NC)

Barnes, Roy A. "Searching for the Monster of Lake Norman." Travel Thru History (travelthruhistory.com). Accessed September 29, 2024.

No author. "Lake Norman Monster Sightings." Lake Norman Monster (lakenormanmonster.com). Accessed September 29, 2024.

No author. "The History of Lake Norman." Visit Lake Norman (visitlakenorman.com). July 30, 2023.

Staff writer. "The Story Behind this North Carolina Lake Will Give You Chills." Only in Your State (onlyinyourstate.com). July 31, 2017.

LAKE HERRINGTON MONSTER

(Herrington Lake, KY)

Coyte, Kaye. "Monster in Lake Herrington: Creature or Catfish?" The Kentucky Kernel (herringtonlakeky.com). February 13, 1974. Reprinted: February 21, 2023.

No author. "A 'Monster' in Kentucky's Herrington Lake?" WBKR 92.5 The Country Station (wbkr.com). Accessed on September 28, 2024.

No author. "Lake Herrington Monster." Cryptid Wiki (cryptidz.fandom.com). Accessed on September 28, 2024.

About Jessica Freeburg

Jessica Freeburg is an internationally published author, history nerd, and researcher of the unexplained. She has written a wide variety of books, ranging from graphic novels to paranormal fiction, as well as nonfiction focused on creepy legends and dark moments from history.

As the founder of Ghost Stories Ink, Jessica has performed paranormal investigations at reportedly haunted locations across the US. She has appeared in documentaries and shows on such networks as the Travel Channel and Amazon Prime—talking about ghosts and haunted places—and can often be heard cohosting the wildly popular podcast *Darkness Radio*.

You can learn more about Jessica's work at jessicafreeburg.com.

About Natalie Fowler

Natalie Fowler, once a practicing attorney, is now an award-winning author and ghost writer. Natalie's published works include nonfiction books on poignant—though sometimes dark—historical events and haunting legends.

She is the researcher and historian for Ghost Stories Ink and has led paranormal investigations at some of the most notoriously haunted locations in the country. Inspired by the concept of spirit rescue, she cofounded a paranormal group called Paranormal Services Cooperative and has published accounts of her work as a medium in this field. You can learn more about her work and publications at nataliefowler.com.

The Story of AdventureKEEN

We are an independent nature and outdoor activity publisher. Our founding dates back more than 40 years, guided then and now by our love of being in the woods and on the water, by our passion for reading and books, and by the sense of wonder and discovery made possible by spending time recreating outdoors in beautiful places.

It is our mission to share that wonder and fun with our readers, especially with those who haven't yet experienced all the physical and mental health benefits that nature and outdoor activity can bring.

#bewellbeoutdoors